John D. Haldane · Englische Redensarten

John D. Haldane

Englische Redensarten

John D. Haldane war für Berlitz Englischlehrer und Schuldirektor in Spanien und England, bevor er für einen deutschen Chemie-Konzern in verschiedenen Führungspositionen tätig war. Im Ruhestand geht er seinen Ambitionen als Autor mit dem Schwerpunkt sprachliche Kommunikation nach.

© Gondrom Verlag GmbH, Bindlach 2007

Covergestaltung: Christine Retz
Coverabbildung: Norbert Zlöbl, Nürnberg

Alle Rechte vorbehalten:
Kein Teil dieses Werkes darf ohne schriftliche Einwilligung des Verlages in irgendeiner Form (Fotokopie, Mikrofilm oder ein anderes Verfahren) reproduziert oder unter Verwendung elektronischer Systeme verarbeitet, vervielfältigt oder verbreitet werden.

013

ISBN 978-3-8112-2856-6

5 4 3 2 1

www.gondrom-verlag.de

Inhalt

Durch Redensarten wird eine Sprache lebendig 8

Animals 13
  Bear, Bird, Bull, Butterfly, Cat, Chicken, Cow, Dog, Duck, Eel, Elephant, Feather, Fish, Fly/Flies, Fox, Goose, Hen, Herring, Hog, Horse, Lamb, Lark, Lion, Monkey, Mouse, Mule, Owl, Peacock, Rat, Sheep, Wolf

Body 21
  Arm, Back, Backbone, Belly, Blood, Body, Bone, Brain, Breast, Cheek, Chest, Chin, Ear, Elbow, Eye, Face, Foot/Feet, Finger, Fingertips, Gall, Guts, Hair, Hand, Head, Heart, Heels, Lap, Leg, Lip, Mouth, Muscle, Neck, Nerve, Nose, Palm, Shoulder, Skin, Stomach, Throat, Thumb, Toe, Tongue, Tooth/Teeth

Clothing 59
  Bag, Belt, Bloomer, Bonnet, Boot, Cap, Cotton, Cuff, Dressed, Glove, Hat, Pants, Pocket, Rag, Shirt, Shoe, Sleeve, Sock, Thread, Trousers, Uppers, Yarn

Colours 64
  Black, Blue, Colour, Green, Pink, Red, White, Yellow

Natural Elements 66
  Air, Cloud, Earth, Element, Fire, Ice, Nature, Ocean, Rain, Storm, Sun, Water, Wind

Food – Drink 70
  Apple, Bacon, Bean, Beef, Bite, Bread, Butter, Cake, Core, Cucumber, Egg, Fat, Fig, Gooseberry, Jam, Loaf, Meal, Meat, Milk, Mustard, Nut, Nutshell, Oil, Peanuts, Peas, Picnic, Pie, Potato, Salt, Sardines, Soup, Stew, Tea

Sports – Games 76
  Back-pedal, Ball, Bat, Bay, Boat, Cards, Catch, Check, Game, Jump, Leap, Lurch, Mark, Peg, Play, Pole, Ring, Rope, Run, Rut, Saddle, Sail, Sport, Spur, Stake, Stream, Stroke, Sweep, Trot

House – Articles 84
Bell, Bottle, Brooms, Brush, Bucket, Candle, Ceiling, Clock, Foundations, Fuel, Gate-post, Home, House, Iron, Kettle, Pan, Path, Picture, Pin, Plate, Pot, Roof, Rug, Shelf, Sieve, Slate, Sponge, Stone, String, Table, Tile, Tooth-comb, Towel, Wall

Illness – Health 91
Accident, Aching, All in, Bag, Bald, Beat, Blind, Bread-line, Cold, Cough, Cropper, Deaf, Doctor, Door, End, Feel, Fit, Ill, Limb, Marrow, Medicine, Pains, Pill, Sick, Sneezed, Thin, Way, Weather, Whacked, Wreck

Life – Death – Luck 95
Age, Blessing, Chance, Dead, Death, Devil, Faith, Ghost, Gospel, Grace, Heaven, Hell, Life, Light, Live, Luck, Mercies, Sake, Save

Mind – Feeling 100
Above, Absence, Actions, Bitten, Bored, Bottom, Breath, Browned, Bygones, Care, Class, Compliments, Conscience, Crystal Ball, Damper, Dawned, Dream, Dumps, Earnest, Excuse, Fancy, Fear, Fed up, Feelings, Get off, Gift, Haste, Hopes, Hue, Idea, Let down, Lie, Loss, Love, Message, Mind, Misery, Outcry, Peace, Point, Pride, Purposes, Qualms, Rage, Ray, Reason, Regret, Ride, Safe, Said, Same, Scent, Sense(s), Shame, Sight, Slow, Sorrows, Steam, Swoop, Tether, Thick, Thing, Thoughts, Top, Tune, Turn, Uptake, Use against, Waste, Way, Well, Wise(r), Wits, Wrong

Character 118
Abreast, Ahead, Bold, Courage, Colours, Cold, Dark, Envy, Exhibition, Insult, Laurels, Lot, Martyr, Mind, Principles, Reputation, Tower, Way

Money – Finance 121
Account, Bargain, Cash, Crown, Dollar, Gold, Mint, Money, Pence, Penny, Ransom, Scrape, Way

Names – Numbers 124
Aleck, Billy, Bob, Count, First, Forty, Half, Halves, Hobson, Jack, Jack Frost, Jack of all trades, Jack Robinson, Jekyll and Hyde,

Mickey, Name(s), Nine, Number, Once, One, Punch, Six(es), Tom, Tom Dick and Harry, Tomboy, Two

Relationship **129**
Ado, Apron-strings, Ass, Baby, Bark, Beauty, Boy, Circle, Coast, Copycat, Decks, Deep end, Family, Father, Flop, Glance, Image, Innocent, Joke/Joking, League, Pop, Put off, Safe, Ship, Spick, Square, Stops, Tale, Terms, Thieves, Trial, Wing

Words **133**
About, All, Alone, Fancy, May, Tip, Wake, Word

Vegetation **137**
Bunch, Bush, Daisy, Hay, Leaf, Log, Root, Rose, Straw, Tree, Wood

Time – Day **139**
Day, Daylight, Month, Time, Tomorrow, Years

Tools **141**
Hook, Jam, Key, Nail, Screw, Spade, Spanner, Tools, Wedge

Town – Country **142**
Bar, Bridge, Corner, Deal, Driver, Hill, Millstone, Mountain, Needle, Road, Robbery, Roost, Street, Town, Track, Trail, Window shopping

World – Places **146**
Cloud-cuckoo-land, Coventry, Dutch, Newcastle, Place, Rome, World

Work – Occupations **149**
Act, Book, Business, Chair, Clue, Come-back, Donkey-work, Fiddle, Fits, Job, Judge, Justice, Law, Limelight, Line, Music, Part, Practice, Print, Queue, Scene, Shop, Show, Song, Stage-fright, Trade, Trick, Way, Work

War – Weapons **157**
Battle, Bomb, Ceremony, Daggers, Fight, Fort, Guns, Hatchet, King, Large, Lock, Match, Punch-up, Scot-free, Shot, Struggle, Target, Trap, Trigger, War-path

Register **161**

Englische Redensarten

Durch Redensarten wird eine Sprache lebendig

Als ich im Jahr 1974 meine erste Arbeitsstelle in Deutschland antrat, hatte ich nach etwa drei Wochen meine erste Begegnung mit den Feinheiten deutscher Redensarten. Seit meiner Kindheit hatte ich, vor allem morgens, immer ein oder zwei winzige Wimpern verloren. Die kleinen Biester landeten stets irgendwo in einer Ecke meiner Augen. Eines Morgens also hing ich wieder einmal mit der Nase am Spiegel in unserem Bürowaschraum, um noch eine dieser kleinen Wimpern zu entfernen. Einer meiner Kollegen stand neben mir, hatte mich aber nicht genau beobachtet, als ich ihm erklärte: *Ich habe was im Auge*. Als er gleich darauf den Raum verließ, antwortete er: „Gut für Sie!" Ich wunderte mich: Hat der denn kein Mitgefühl? Erst später wurde mir die übertragene Bedeutung dieses Ausdrucks erklärt: etwas beabsichtigen oder vorhaben. Ob er sich damals überlegte, ob ich *alle Tassen im Schrank hätte* – dessen bin ich mir bis heute nicht sicher ...

Für einen Muttersprachler sind Redensarten selbstverständlicher und fester Bestandteil der Sprache. Englische und deutsche Redensarten werden bereits von Kindheit an in der Familie und im Freundeskreis vermittelt. Im Schulunterricht oder in Sprachkursen für Erwachsene spielen Redensarten allerdings nur eine untergeordnete Rolle oder werden oft gar nicht betrachtet.

Eine Sammlung von Redensarten – wie Sie sie in diesem Buch vorfinden – ist für den deutschen Leser aus diesem Grund umso wichtiger. Die ausgewählten englischen Redensarten sollen als Hilfe für (Sprach-)Schüler dienen, aber auch für Fortgeschrittene, die einen „Blackout" im Gespräch vermeiden und ihre Sprachkenntnisse zusätzlich mit umgangssprachlichen Redewendungen *aufpeppen* wollen.

Was sind überhaupt Redensarten?

Redensarten sind feste sprachliche Einheiten oder Ausdrücke, deren Gesamtbedeutung sich oft nur schwer (oder gar nicht) aus den Bedeutungen der Einzelwörter ableiten lässt. Denn neben ihrer ersten, rein wörtlichen Bedeutung hat jede Redensart auch eine zweite, idiomatische Bedeutung – die eigentlich gemeinte Bedeutung.

Nehmen wir als Beispiel die englische Redewendung *get the bird*. Diese Redewendung hat zwei mögliche Bedeutungen:

1. wörtliche Bedeutung = den Vogel fangen/kriegen

2. idiomatische, sinngemäße Bedeutung = ausgepfiffen werden

Mit ihrer rein wörtlichen Bedeutung haben Redensarten oftmals kaum noch etwas zu tun – oder es scheint zumindest so. So mutet die Redewendung *it's raining cats and dogs* zunächst etwas seltsam an. Sie hat ihren Ursprung in der Mythologie, in der die Katze – so glaubte man – einen großen Einfluss auf das Wetter hatte. So sollen Hexen, die mit ihrem Besen auf den Stürmen geritten seien, die Gestalt von Katzen gehabt haben. Ganz ähnlich verhält es sich mit dem Hund, der als Wärter oder Diener des Sturmgottes Odin galt.

Im Deutschen gibt es für die Redewendung *it's raining cats and dogs* keine direkte Übersetzung, aber es gibt sinngemäße Entsprechungen. Die geläufige Übersetzung ist: *Es gießt in Strömen/wie aus Eimern* (oder: *aus Kübeln* bzw. *aus Kannen*). Andere sagen: *Es schüttet wie blöd/wie verrückt* – was wiederum eher den englischen Redensarten *it's pouring down* oder *chucking it down* (oder derb: *it's pissing down*) entspricht. Darüber hinaus gibt es weitere, weniger bekannte deutsche Varianten wie *Es regnet Bindfäden/Strippen* oder *Es gießt wie mit Mollen* oder sogar *Es regnet junge Hunde*. Redewendungen bringen damit auch immer eine besondere Eigenschaft jeder Sprache zum Ausdruck: Erst durch sie wird eine Sprache wirklich lebendig.

Was Ihnen dieses Buch bietet

Wer ein lebendiges Englisch sprechen möchte, kommt an den typischen englischen Redensarten nicht vorbei. Dieses Buch bietet Ihnen eine repräsentative Sammlung von Redensarten, die in der englischen Sprache von der Mehrheit der Bevölkerung am häufigsten verwendet werden. Der Schwerpunkt dieses Buches liegt auf Redewendungen, darüber hinaus wurden aber auch oft verwendete Sprichwörter oder umgangssprachliche Ausdrücke ausgewählt.

Ein nach Hauptgruppen geordnetes Inhaltsverzeichnis und ein umfassendes, alphabetisch geordnetes Register ermöglichen Ihnen eine schnelle Orientierung durch Kategorien und Themen mit Hilfe deutscher Entsprechungen englischer Redensarten. Ob für die Schule, die Universität, für die Arbeit oder unterwegs mit Auto, Bus, Bahn oder Flugzeug – im handlichen Pocket-Format können Sie dieses Buch überall mitnehmen, Sie können schnell die gesuchten Redensarten nachschlagen oder auch einfach mal zwischendurch darin schmökern.

Jede englische Redensart in diesem Buch wird mit ihren möglichen Variationen oder Alternativen und einem Anwendungsbeispiel vorgestellt. Die Eintragungen in diesem Buch sind wie folgt aufgebaut:

be like a cat on hot bricks *auf glühenden Kohlen sitzen* **V:** like a cat on a hot tin roof **A:** be extremely uneasy **B:** When Jack arrived at the hospital, and the doctor informed him that his wife had just given birth to quintets, he was like a cat on hot bricks.

1. englische Redewendung

2. entsprechende deutsche Redewendung bzw. die geläufige Übersetzung der englischen Redewendung

3. Variation V (wenn vorhanden) zur englischen Redewendung.

Durch Redensarten wird eine Sprache lebendig

Unter einer Variation wird eine *sprachlich* ähnliche Variante zu der aufgeführten Redewendung verstanden.

4. Alternative A zur englischen Redewendung.
   Unter der Alternative A wird eine zwar sprachlich unterschiedliche, aber *sinngemäß* entsprechende Übersetzung der englischen Redewendung verstanden.

Abkürzungen

Wie in der gesprochenen Sprache werden die englischen Abkürzungen in diesem Buch grundsätzlich verwendet:

I am = I'm, I have = I've, I have got = I've got, I had oder I would = I'd, I will/shall = I'll, he is = he's, we are = we're

I did not = I didn't, He has not = He hasn't, He is not = He's not or He isn't, you are not = you aren't or you're not, I have not = I haven't, I cannot = I can't, I could not = I couldn't, I must not = I mustn't, I was not = I wasn't, they were not = they weren't, I will not = I won't, I would not = I wouldn't

---

5. Beispielsatz B: eine praktische Anwendung der englischen Redensart, die eine Situation oder kleine Geschichte schildert, aus der die Bedeutung der Redewendung deutlich wird.

So finden Sie die Redensart, die Sie suchen

Dieses Buch bietet Ihnen zwei Möglichkeiten, eine englische Redensart zu finden. Nehmen wir als Beispiel die englische Redewendung *be like a cat on hot bricks*. Diese Redewendung finden Sie

1. über das Inhaltsverzeichnis. Hier sind die englischen Redensarten nach ihren Hauptwörtern (zum Beispiel „Cat" – Katze) in

alphabetischer Reihenfolge in entsprechenden Hauptgruppen (zum Beispiel „Animals" – Tiere) geordnet.

2. über das deutschsprachige Register: Hier sind die deutschen Entsprechungen der englischen Redewendungen in alphabetischer Reihenfolge geordnet. Ähnlich wie die englischen Redensarten sind auch die deutschen Redewendungen nach ihren Hauptwörtern aufgelistet. Die deutsche Redewendung *auf glühenden Kohlen sitzen* finden Sie entsprechend unter dem Buchstaben K wie Kohlen. Der Seitenverweis führt sie dann automatisch zu der englischen Redewendung.

Generell gilt:

1. Enthält die Redensart ein Substantiv (wie „cat"), finden Sie sie unter diesem Wort.

2. Enthält die Redensart zwei Substantive (zum Beispiel „cat" und „bricks"), findet man sie unter dem ersten oder (hinsichtlich der übertragenen Bedeutung der Redensart) dem wichtigeren zweiten Wort (also „cat")

3. Gleichzeitig ist die Hauptgruppe (zum Beispiel „Animal") das ausschlaggebende Kriterium für die Zuordnung der Redensart.

Und jetzt: *Broaden your mind and have fun!*

ANIMALS

BEAR

be like a bear with a sore head *ein richtiger Brummbär sein* **A:** be in a stinking mood **B:** After Jack had lost 10.000 Euros on the stock exchange, he was like a bear with a sore head all week.

BIRD

be as free as a bird (again) *(wieder) frei atmen können* **A:** be/feel free to come and go as one pleases **B:** After 10 years of being married to her violent husband, she finally divorced him and felt as free as a bird again.

get the bird *ausgepfiffen werden* **V:** give someone the bird **A:** get a boo **B:** We went to the theatre to see the new comedy, but the acting was so disastrous that at the end of the performance the whole cast got the bird.

the early bird catches the worm *wer zuerst kommt, mahlt zuerst* **A:** first come, first served **B:** Jack was at the shop door at 5 in the morning, and got the only television for half price. – That's life, the early bird catches the worm.

A bird in the hand is worth two in the bush *lieber den Spatz in der Hand als die Taube auf dem Dach* **B:** The top hotel in Berlin has offered me an interview for a job as Director, should I accept it? – Forget it, you've been assistant manager at your present hotel for only a year, you won't have chance, be realistic – a bird in the hand is worth two in the bush.

a little bird told me *Das hat mir jemand im Vertrauen gesagt, das hat mir ein Vögelchen gezwitschert* **A:** someone told me in confidence **B:** How did you know that our director has promoted me to head of department? – A little bird told me.

kill two birds with one stone *zwei Fliegen mit einer Klappe schlagen* **A:** do them both at the same time **B:** I've got to collect your mother from the station this evening. I can kill two birds with one stone, and also buy the train tickets for our holiday.

BULL

be like a bull in a china shop *wie ein Elefant im Porzellanladen* **A:** be or act clumsily and destructively **B:** In the library, Jack knocked down a stand full of video cassettes, then the librarian told him to leave for being like a bull in a china shop.

cock and bull story *ein Ammenmärchen* **A:** an old wife's tale **B:** Fred came to return the money I'd lent him, and he told me some cock and bull story about a man robbing him of all his money on his way to my house.

take the bull by the horns *den Stier bei den Hörnern packen* **A:** face up to a difficult task **B:** He had spent weeks thinking about asking for a salary increase, then he finally took the bull by horns, and walked into his boss's office and asked for a rise.

that's bullshit *Das ist Scheiße/ Bockmist* **A:** crap **B:** I haven't got a hope of passing the interview – That's bullshit, George, you've had the same training as the others, think positive and the job's yours.

BUTTERFLY

have butterflies in one's stomach *Lampenfieber haben* **A:** have stage fright **B:** Even experienced theatrical actors still have butterflies in their stomach on the opening night.

CAT

no room to swing a cat *kaum Platz haben, sich zu rühren* **A:** be cramped up **B:** It may be a 5 star hotel, darling, but our bedroom is so small, there is no room to swing a cat.

grin like a cheshire cat *wie ein Honigkuchenpferd grinsen* **A:** grin from ear to ear **B:** Just because I left the eggs in boiling water for 15 minutes, there's no need to grin like a Cheshire cat.

play cat and mouse with someone *mit jemandem Katz und Maus spielen* **A:** play around with someone **B:** Do you think Jack's new girl friend is as sincere as Jack is about their relationship? – No, she's dangerous, she's just playing cat and mouse with him.

let the cat out of the bag *die Katze aus dem Sack lassen* **A:** disclose a secret **B:** You shouldn't have told my wife I was at the jeweller's yesterday. She can guess now what I'm giving her for her birthday, you let the cat out of the bag!

be like a cat on hot bricks *auf glühenden Kohlen sitzen* **V:** like a cat on a hot tin roof **A:** be extremely uneasy **B:** When Jack arrived at the hospital, and the doctor informed him that his wife had just given birth to quintets, he was like a cat on hot bricks.

curiosity killed the cat *Neugierige Leute sterben früh* **A:** being over curious can often lead one into trouble **B:** When Jack leaned out of the window to see what was going on in his neighbour's garden, he lost balance and fell out of the window, fortunately into the pool – Well, curiosity killed the cat.

CHICKEN

chicken out (of something) *kneifen* **A:** back out of something **B:** On his first visit as a voluntary worker for the disabled, the handicapped people made him so upset that he chickened out and gave in his resignation.

be chicken-feed *'n Appel und 'n Ei* **A:** not be worth talking about **B:** As a nurse, Susan is working often more than 12 hours a day, including night shifts, but compared with the surgeons her salary is chicken-feed.

don't count your chickens before they are hatched *Man soll den Tag nicht vor dem Abend loben* **A:** don't bet on it yet **B:** Jack was sure his uncle would leave him a lot of money in his will, but he didn't get a penny – Well, you shouldn't count your chickens before they're hatched.

COW

till the cows come home *bis in alle Ewigkeit* **A:** until one is blue in the face **B:** You can argue with Jack on his communistic views till the cows come home, you won't change his opinion.

DOG

be a lucky dog *ein Glückspilz sein* **V:** (women = lucky bitch) **A:** be very lucky **B:** He's neither good-looking nor has an interesting character, but all the girls flock on him – the lucky dog.

You can't teach an old dog new tricks *Was Hänschen nicht lernt, lernt Hans nimmermehr* **A:** if he hasn't learnt now, he never will

ANIMALS

B: The older members of staff are against working with the computer – that's understandable, you can't teach an old dog new tricks!

to be a dog in the manger *ein Spielverderber sein* **A:** a real spoil-sport **B:** Jack, you can walk normally again after your accident last year, could my son borrow your crutches, he's sprained his knee playing football? – No, I may have an accident again – Well, you're a dog in the manger.

Let sleeping dogs lie *Schlafende Hunde soll man nicht wecken* **A:** don't stir up the past **B:** Even though John married you last year, you're still mentioning his ex-wife, you know that upsets him, let sleeping dogs lie.

DUCK

be a sitting duck *leichte Beute sein* **A:** be in a vulnerable position **B:** The terrorist was a sitting duck for the special force, who had surrounded the building and had 5 marksmen focused on him.

be a dead duck *kalter Kaffee sein* **A:** be ancient history **B:** Why don't we offer our product in smaller packets for single people. The idea is a dead duck, the competition started years ago.

EEL

as slippery as an eel *glatt wie ein Aal* **A:** be always wriggling one's way out **B:** Jack was as slippery as an eel, and answered the lawyer's questions so cleverly that he convinced the jury he was innocent.

ELEPHANT

memory like an elephant *ein Gedächtnis wie ein Elefant haben* **A:** have a long memory **B:** When I asked him if I could borrow his bike, he refused and told me I had taken his bike without asking when we were at school 30 years ago – Incredible, he must have a memory like an elephant!

FEATHER

could have knocked someone down with a feather *wie vom Donner gerührt sein* **A:** be totally surprised or flabbergasted **B:** When I told my wife we'd won 6 Million on the lottery, you could have knocked her down with a feather.

that's a feather in one's cap *ein Ruhmesblatt für jemanden sein* **A:** that does someone credit **B:** That's a feather in his cap, becoming a permanent member of the school's football team, after training with them only twice.

FISH

a big fish *ein großes Tier* **A:** a very important person **B:** Be careful what you say at our office party to Tim Smith, he's a big fish from the US corporate offices.

feel like a fish out of water *sich wie ein Fisch auf dem Trockenen fühlen* **A:** feel out of one's element **B:** After 15 years flying with the Air Force, he was suddenly transferred to the Army, and felt like a fish out of water.

a small fish *ein kleiner Fisch* **A:** an unimportant person **B:** I wouldn't speak to the manager of your department about a salary increase, he's only a small fish in the company, I'd go straight to the divisional director.

take to it like (a) fish to water *sich fühlen wie ein Fisch im Wasser* **A:** feel immediately at home **B:** After 2 years theatrical training, how did Susan get on in her first TV film role? – She's got acting in her blood, she took to it like a fish to water.

drink like a fish *saufen wie ein Loch* **A:** be a hard drinker **B:** I wouldn't let Jack drive you home after the office party, he drinks like a fish.

that smells/sounds/looks fishy *jemandem verdächtig/spanisch vorkommen* **A:** look very suspicious **B:** That house insurance which the new company offered you smells fishy, it's far too cheap, I'd compare offers from 2 or 3 other companies.

FLY / FLIES

there are no flies on him *den kann man nicht hinters Licht führen* **A:** be too clever to be deceived **B:** You're wasting your time, if you try to sell that old car to Jim, he'll notice the repairs needed immediately, there are no flies on him.

couldn't hurt a fly *keiner Fliege etwas zuleide tun können* **A:** wouldn't harm anyone **B:** He denied having murdered the child,

ANIMALS

and emphasised again that he couldn't hurt a fly.

a fly in the ointment *ein Haar in der Suppe* **A:** be just enough to spoil it **B:** I was looking forward to our holiday in Spain, but we have a fly in the ointment now, we'll have to take my grumbling aunt with us.

FOX

as cunning/sly as a fox *schlau wie ein Fuchs* **A:** be clever **B:** So Jack offered you 500 pounds for your car; I'd look for other buyers, Jack's as cunning as a fox, he'll sell your car for double the price he's paid.

GOOSE

cook one's own goose *den Ast absägen, auf dem man sitzt* **A:** ruin one's own existence **B:** His father-in-law was about to pass his company over to him, when he had an affair with another woman – he's cooked his own goose now.

not say boo to a goose *ein Hasenfuß sein* **A:** not make the mildest protest **B:** Jack's wife wants her parents to live with them in their small flat – Jack won't say a word, he wouldn't say boo to a goose.

kill the goose that lays the golden egg *das Huhn, das goldene Eier legt, schlachten* **A:** bite the hand that feeds you **B:** Jack has inherited his father's company at the age of 30, and wants to sell it. – He's stupid, he shouldn't kill the goose that lays the golden egg.

HEN

be hen-pecked *unter dem Pantoffel stehen* **A:** the wife wears the trousers at home **B:** No wonder Jack is hen-pecked by his wife, she found out he had an affair with another woman.

HERRING

red herring *ein Ablenkungsmanöver* **A:** divert attention from the main question **B:** When the government heard the terrorists were now attacking Buckingham Palace instead of London airport, they fortunately took it as a red herring, and captured them in the luggage area of the airport.

HOG

go the whole hog *aufs Ganze gehen* **A:** stick it out to the (very) end **B:** In spite of a sprained ankle after 10 miles of the marathon, he went the whole hog and finished the race in third position.

HORSE

be a dark horse *ein unbeschriebenes Blatt sein* **A:** be not well known **B:** You were right about John being a dark horse, he took part in our golf tournament, saying he had only played a few games, and won the first prize!

put the cart before the horse *das Pferd beim Schwanze aufzäumen* **A:** finish the first step before taking the second step **B:** We should book our holiday now, in 3 months we should have saved enough money. – I wouldn't put the cart before the horse, I'd book after you've saved at least half.

back the wrong horse *aufs falsche Pferd setzen* **A:** make the wrong decision **B:** He backed the wrong horse buying shares in that computer company, it went bankrupt last week.

work like a horse *wie ein Pferd arbeiten* **A:** work his nose to the grindstone **B:** Jack's wife must be happy that he installed the cupboards in their bedroom. – Yes, he worked like a horse all afternoon, but he's in hospital now with back problems.

eat like a horse *fressen wie ein Scheunendrescher* **V:** be so hungry, I could eat a horse **A:** scoff it down **B:** After being trapped underground at the coal mine for 3 days, when he was rescued he ate like a horse.

flog a dead horse *sich vergeblich anstrengen* **A:** waste one's time **B:** John is a devoted catholic, there's no point trying to convince him that abortion is in certain cases acceptable, you'll be flogging a dead horse.

Hold your horses! *Nicht so schnell! Immer mit der Ruhe!* **V:** hold your reins **A:** wait a moment **B:** Hold your horses! I wasn't to blame for hitting the dog, the owner should have had the dog on the lead, then it wouldn't have jumped out onto the road.

LAMB

take something like a lamb *etwas geduldig wie ein Lamm*

ANIMALS

ertragen **A:** accept something without any resistence or fuss **B:** When Peter had to move out of his room he'd been renting from my father, because his sister needed it, he didn't make a scene and took it like a lamb.

as meek as a lamb *sanft wie ein Lamm* **V:** as gentle as a lamb **A:** be as gentle as a dove **B:** Jack couldn't do that job as a bouncer at the disco club, he's as meek as a lamb.

LARK

be up with the lark *mit den Hühnern aufstehen* **A:** get up at the break/crack of dawn, **B:** John is up with the lark every morning, he jogs for an hour, spends time on his painting and has a relaxing breakfast with his wife before going to the office.

LION

lion's share *der Löwenanteil* **A:** largest part/share **B:** Mother told her eldest son to cut the cake into 3 equal portions, but he took the lion's share and left two small pieces for his brothers.

as brave as a lion *mutig wie ein Löwe* **A:** be a brave warrior **B:** After jumping into the stormy sea to save a young child from drowning, the local press complimented John on being as brave as a lion.

MONKEY

make a monkey (out) of someone *jemanden zum Narren halten* **A:** make someone look/feel ridiculous **B:** You made a right monkey of me, telling our guests that my meal was burning. If you do that again, I won't cook anymore and we'll go out for a meal.

MOUSE

be (as) poor as a church mouse *arm wie eine Kirchenmaus sein* **A:** not have a penny **B:** You can't ask Philip to join us for a meal in that exclusive French restaurant, you know he's as poor as a church mouse.

MULE

stubborn as a mule *störrisch wie ein Esel* **A:** be pig-headed or stiff-necked **B:** We must tell Jack, we have to cancel our planned holiday due to the outbreak of cholera – Forget it, he's as stubborn as a mule, he'd still go, even if there were a war on there.

OWL

be as wise as an (old) owl *weise wie eine Eule* **A:** be old and wise **B:** Your grandfather is the best one to help you with your legal problem, he spent 40 years as a top judge, he's a wise as an (old) owl.

PEACOCK

proud as a peacock *stolz wie ein Pfau/Spanier* **V:** proud as a Spaniard **A:** (positive) be justifiably proud of one's achievements, (negative, seldom) be conceited and vain **B:** She financed the whole training course herself by working evenings in the super market; when she finally received her diploma she was proud as a peacock.

RAT

smell a rat *Lunte riechen, den Braten riechen* **A:** smell/sense danger **B:** Judy smelt a rat, when Jack kept on postponing the wedding, then she found out that he'd had an affair with another woman for the last 7 months.

SHEEP

separate the sheep from the goats *die Schafe von den Böcken trennen* **A:** separate the good from the bad **B:** The police took 20 youths suspected of drug dealing to the police station, but the hearing took some time, it was difficult to separate the sheep from the goats.

WOLF

keep the wolf from the door *jemanden über Wasser halten* **A:** keep someone's head above water **B:** Amazing how George keeps the wolf from the door, with his low paid job his family still have all the essentials in life.

BODY

ARM

one would give one's right arm *alles darum geben* **A:** would give anything/the world to **B:** My father died very young, I'd give my right arm just to be able to see him once more.

be someone's right arm *seine/ihre rechte Hand sein* **A:** be the most trusted supporter and helper **B:** Since our boss hired that

BODY

young assistant, they appear together at all meetings – Yes, the boss won't do anything without him, the young man is his right arm.

do something with one arm tied behind one's back *etwas mit links machen* **A:** do something with one's eyes shut or standing on one's head **B:** I wouldn't tell your new neighbour his radio is too loud, he's an ex-boxer – if you get into a fight, he'd beat you with one arm tied behind his back.

keep someone at arm's length *sich jemanden vom Leibe/auf Distanz halten* **A:** keep someone at a distance **B:** If you're going to the cinema for the first time with Jack tonight, then keep him at arm's length, he's a passionate Casanova.

greet someone with open arms *jemanden mit offenen Armen empfangen* **A:** greet/welcome someone with out-stretched hands/arms **B:** When the Beatles returned from their US tour, the prime minister greeted them with open arms, their music exports had helped the British economy.

BACK

have someone on one's back *jemanden am Hals haben* **A:** have someone round one's neck **B:** The holiday was strenuous, I had my mother-in-law on my back the whole two weeks, my wife could have taken her for at least one day.

scratch my back and I'll scratch yours *eine Hand wäscht die andere* **A:** if you help me, I'll help you **B:** Could I borrow your car tomorrow? – Well (if) you scratch my back, I'll scratch yours, you can have the car, but can you lend me your garden mower for the weekend?

put one's back into something *sich in etwas hineinknien* **A:** get a move on **B:** You said in July you could decorate the walls and ceilings in a month, if you don't put your back into it, we're still be sitting on paint tins at Christmas.

break one's back *sich abrackern* **A:** overdo things **Vulg:** work one's arse off. **B:** He broke his back building up his company; then his two sons took over and the company was bankrupt within a year.

glad to see the back/last of someone *sich freuen, jemanden von hinten zu sehen* **A:** be happy that someone has left or gone **B:** After your mother's 2 week stay with us, I must admit, after her continual criticism, that I'm glad to see the back of her.

be (flat) on one's back *flachliegen* **A:** be ill in bed **B:** John won't be playing football for the rest of the season, he's (flat) on his back with a broken leg.

get one's own back *sich rächen* **A:** take revenge **B:** Poor Jim, his nasty neighbours let the air out of the front tyres of his car. But Jim got his own back by filling up their half empty petrol tank with water.

do it behind one's back *etwas hinter jemandes Rücken tun* **A:** do something without someone knowing **B:** Don't invite George to your party, he's been criticising you behind your back for weeks.

turn one's back on someone *jemandem den Rücken zudrehen* **A:** have nothing more to do with someone **B:** No wonder the director turned his back on you at the office party, he hasn't forgotten you severely criticized him in front of our best customer.

have one's back to the wall *mit dem Rücken an der Wand stehen, in die Enge getrieben sein* **V:** be with one's back to the wall **A:** see no alternative **B:** Saddam Hussein had his back to the wall, as the USA were searching for weapons of mass destruction and threatening to invade Irak.

get off one's back *jemanden in Ruhe lassen* **A:** leave someone in peace/alone **B:** I'm fed up with your criticisms for the last hour, get off my back!

give someone a pat on the back *jemandem auf die Schulter klopfen* **V:** you deserve a pat on the back **A:** congratulate someone **B:** When Jack came home and told his parents he'd failed the exam, his father knew how much he had studied, and still gave him a pat on the back.

BACKBONE

have no backbone *kein Rückgrat haben* **A:** lack self-confidence or willpower **B:** The way Peter's

BODY

wife and children order him around is one thing, but he also lets his secretary make all the decisions, he's simply got no backbone.

BELLY

have one's (a) bellyful *die Nase voll von etwas/jemandem haben* **V:** have a basinful **A:** have/do more than enough **B:** Our top surgeon left the hospital this afternoon, is he ill? – No, he's had his/a bellyful, he's been operating non-stop for the last 48 hours.

BLOOD

make one's blood boil *das Blut in den Adern zum Kochen bringen* **A:** make one furious **B:** After our mother's funeral, it made my blood boil seeing my brother searching her handbags and clothing for money.

make one's blood run cold *Es läuft jemandem eiskalt über den Rücken* **V:** chill one's blood **A:** shock/scare one to death **B:** As Jill left the disco late at night, two youths with knives suddenly appeared and made her blood run cold, fortunately the police were nearby.

blood is thicker than water *Blut ist dicker als Wasser* **B:** Tom had been promised the job as director, then the boss suddenly gave the position to his son; as they say „blood is thicker than water".

it runs in the blood *jemandem liegt etwas im Blut* **A:** be inherited **B:** His father was great footballer, and now young John has been selected for the national team, it must run in the blood.

sweat blood *Blut und Wasser schwitzen* **A:** work under severe pressure **B:** Don't waste your time inviting George to your birthday on Saturday, he's sweating blood trying to finish his report after being ill for two weeks.

do/act in cold blood *kaltblütig handeln* **A:** do without remorse or feeling **B:** His lawyer argued that Jack had killed his wife in a drunken and unstable state, but the jury decided he had acted in cold blood and he was sentenced to life imprisonment.

be after one's blood *jemandem an den Kragen wollen* **V:** be out for one's blood **A:** want to get one's hands on someone **B:** I'd leave the country before Jack returns from holiday; when he sees you've ruined his sports car, he'll be after your blood.

BODY

over my dead body *Nur über meine Leiche* **A:** you'll have to kill me first **B:** If that scoundrel wants to marry my daughter, then it will be over my dead body.

BONE

have a bone to pick with someone *mit jemandem ein Hühnchen zu rupfen haben* **A:** have a barney to pick with you **B:** I have a bone to pick with you young lad, I saw you take some money out of mummy's purse this morning.

a bone of contention *ein Zankapfel* **A:** have reason for dispute **B:** It was a bone of contention between the two brothers, when their father died and left everything to the elder son.

make no bones about it *nicht viel Federlesen machen* **A:** do something without any qualms **B:** When Jack's girl friend invited him to meet her parents, Lord and Lady Camway, he was asked about his family's background; he made no bones about it, and said his father is working class.

feel something in one's bones *etwas im Gespür haben* **A:** have a feeling something will happen **B:** Susan shouldn't have flown today; an accident is likely to occur, I can't explain it, but I can feel it in my bones.

BRAIN

rack one's brains (out) on *sich den Kopf über etwas zerbrechen* **A:** concentrate deeply on something **B:** The scientist racked his brains the whole night on trying to find the solution, but by the morning he was none the wiser.

BREAST

make a clean breast (of something) *sich etwas von der Seele reden* **A:** take it out your system **B:** The boss suspects you were involved in losing our best customer, you ought to make a clean breast of things, and tell him the truth.

BODY

CHEEK

don't give me any of your cheek *Sei nicht so frech zu mir* **V:** none of your cheek **A:** none of your lip **B:** Don't give me any of your cheek, I've been finance director with our company for 20 years, first learn the basics, then you can make constructive suggestions.

have a/the cheek *die Frechheit haben* **V:** note grammatical difference in 2 examples a/the cheek **A:** be cheeky **B:** Our new secretary has <u>a</u> cheek, when I was introduced to her she asked me for a loan. She had the cheek to ask me for a loan.

turn the other cheek *die andere Wange hinhalten* **A:** turn the other side **B:** He'd been tortured in a prison camp during the war, and when the hooligans hit him to the ground and stole his money, he felt sorry for them and turned the other cheek.

CHEST

get something off one's chest *seinem Herzen Luft machen, sich etwas von der Seele reden* **A:** get it out of your system **B:** I can see you're very worried, tell me about your problem, that often helps to get it off your chest.

CHIN

keep one's chin up *die Ohren steif halten* **V:** keep one's pecker up, Short form: Chin up! **A:** keep on top **B:** I know your instructors are not so experienced, but keep your chin up, and learn the most from situation, and I'm sure you'll pass the final exam.

EAR

have a good ear for something *ein feines Ohr/Gehör für etwas haben* **A:** have a good feeling for something **B:** Experienced doctors have a good ear for telling when a patient is not telling the truth. She's got a good ear for music.

go in/through one ear and out the other *zum einem Ohr hinein, zum andern (wieder) hinaus* **A:** turn a deaf ear **B:** Did you tell David he shouldn't go sailing today, because of the bad weather? – Of course I did, but he's a keen sailor, it went in one ear and out the other.

turn a deaf ear (to) *sich taub stellen* **A:** make out he was deaf,

B: When his mother started scolding him for not clearing up his room, he turned a deaf ear and continued his computer game.

a word in someone's ear *ein Wort im Vertrauen* **A:** just a word (or a little word) in your ear **B:** A word in your ear, George, before you leave the office party, you've been recommended as successor to the vice-president.

be all ear(s) *ganz Ohr sein* **A:** pay attention **B:** Jack was bored hearing about George's problems, then John came into the pub and said he had a new joke, then Jack was all ears.

be still wet behind the ears *noch grün hinter den Ohren sein* **A:** be unexperienced or naive **B:** Our daughter has been offered a job in Saudi Arabia, what do you think? – No way, she's still wet behind the ears, and could land into trouble.

be up to one's ears in (debt) *bis über die/über beide Ohren in (Schulden) stecken* **V:** be up to the ears in work/problems **A:** be up to one's eyes, eyeballs, neck in **B:** Forget about asking John to come on holiday with us this year, he couldn't afford it, he's up to his ears in debt.

can't believe one's ears *seinen Ohren nicht trauen* **B:** When the organisers rang and told me I'd won the first prize of two weeks in the Bahamas, I couldn't believe my ears.

come/get to one's ears *jemandem zu Ohren kommen* **A:** come to one's knowledge **B:** It has come to my ears that you wish to leave your present company, my company has an interesting position vacant, could we meet to discuss details?

prick up one's ears *die Ohren spitzen* **B:** During the interview for the job, he listened to the work involved with interest, but pricked up his ears when he heard the high salary.

ELBOW

elbow one's way through *seine Ellbogen gebrauchen* **A:** push the opposition aside **B:** His director was not very impressed with him, but he elbowed his way through, and after 5 years became a board member.

BODY

be up to the elbows in *bis zum Hals in (zum Beispiel Arbeit) stecken* **A:** up to one's eyes, eyeballs, neck **B:** When he returned from holiday, he was up to the elbows in work, because his two colleagues had resigned while he was away.

EYE

turn a blind eye to something *ein Auge/beide Augen zudrücken* **A:** close an eye to something **B:** The manager was impressed with new girl at the cash-desk, so when she got annoyed with a customer, he turned a blind eye to the incident.

someone/thing catches the eye of someone *jemandem ins Auge fallen* **A:** attract someone's attention **B:** At the beauty contest, Mary immediately caught the eye of the judge with her splendid figure. The quality difference in the two carpets caught his eye immediately.

not to take an eye off someone *seine Augen nicht von jemandem/etwas lassen* **A:** keep a sharp eye on someone **B:** When we wanted to leave the party, the hostess's dog followed and didn't take an eye off us, until we'd closed the door behind us.

keep an eye on someone *jemanden/etwas im Auge behalten* **A:** keep him under your eye **B:** In view of his past records, after the criminal was released from prison, the police still kept an eye on him.

have an eye (a good eye) for something *ein (das) Auge für etwas haben* **A:** have the right judgement/feeling **B:** Mary came back from the sales with beautiful clothes at half the price. Yes, she certainly has an eye for bargains.

do something with an eye to *etwas tun in Hinblick auf, etwas im Auge haben* **V:** have his eye on doing **A:** do something with the objective/aim of doing **B:** She studied French with an eye to getting a job in a fashion house in Paris. He's had his eye on buying that cottage for months.

not have eyes in the back of one's head *hinten keine Augen im Kopf haben* **A:** can't see from behind **B:** How do you expect me to have seen you come rushing round the corner, when I was facing the other way, I haven't got eyes in the back of my head, you know!

see someone/thing with a different eye *jemanden/etwas mit anderen Augen sehen* **A:** see someone in a different light **B:** After three weeks in a small ship with my two friends, I saw them with a totally different eye – our friendship has just ended!

have only have eyes for one person *nur Augen für einen/eine haben* **A:** have only one person in mind/on one's mind **B:** Since the first lesson with the new young female maths teacher, Fred has only eyes for her. He's even taken interest in maths suddenly!

have eyes like a hawk *Augen wie ein Luchs haben* **A:** see extraordinarily well **B:** Trying to smuggle a laptop out of the firm is not worth a try, the security officers controlling the front entrance have eyes like a hawk.

not have eyes in one's head *keine Augen im Kopf haben* **A:** not careful/alert **B:** That's the second time you've driven over the crossing when the traffic lights were red, haven't you got any eyes in your head?

see with the naked eye *mit bloßem Auge erkennen* **A:** see something by oneself/alone **B:** On a clear day, you can see the white cliffs of Dover from the French coast with the naked eye.

not believe one's own eyes *seinen Augen nicht trauen* **V:** with „can't/couldn't" or „be unable to" **B:** After your wife had that face lift, I couldn't believe my own eyes – she looked 20 years younger.

see with one's own eyes *etwas mit eigenen Augen sehen* **A:** witness/see something alone/oneself (Note: eye-witness = Augenzeuge) **B:** I'm sorry Jack, but your son was unfortunately involved in the bank robbery. I saw him with my own eyes, when he came out of the bank with his friends.

keep one's eyes skinned *die Augen offen halten* **V:** keep your eyes peeled **A:** keep your eyes open **B:** As Susan left the disco

BODY

with her girl friend at midnight, she told her to keep her eyes skinned for strangers when they went through the park.

give someone the eye *jemandem verliebte Augen machen* **A:** make eyes at someone **B:** The head waiter was immediately fired, when the manager caught him giving his wife the eye in front of the guests.

not be able to look someone in the eye *jemandem nicht in die Augen sehen können* **V:** can't look him (straight) in the face **A:** not make eye contact with **B:** When the police brought the drunken youth back home, he couldn't look his father (straight) in the eye.

open one's eyes to something *jemandem die Augen öffnen* **A:** make someone aware of the fact/truth **B:** Jack's wife had been having a relationship with another man for some months, and then I opened his eyes to his wife's unfaithfulness.

shut one's eyes to something *die Augen vor etwas verschließen* **A:** close one's eyes to something **B:** Most men shut their eyes to the fact, that women drivers cause fewer accidents than men.

one's eyes are bigger than one's stomach *Die Augen sind größer als der Mund* **V:** bigger than your belly **A:** take more than one can eat **B:** If you hadn't taken such a large portion of ice cream, then you wouldn't have left half of it on your plate. Your eyes are bigger than your stomach.

cry one's eyes out *sich die Augen ausweinen* **V:** cry one's heart out **B:** When the Vet told Susie that her dog had to be put to sleep, she cried her eyes out.

scratch (or would love to scratch) someone's eyes out *jemandem die Augen auskratzen* **A:** be furious with someone (generally used among women) **B:** After catching my husband in bed with the cleaning women, I'd love to scratch her eyes out.

be a feast for the eyes *jemandem eine Augenweide sein* **A:** be a sight for sore eyes **B:** You should have seen the winner of the „Miss World Contest" on TV, with her perfect figure and lovely

Eye

face, she was a feast for the eyes.

be a sight for sore eyes *jemandem eine Augenweide sein* **A:** be a feast for the eyes **B:** You should have seen my wife coming out of the beauty salon, she was a sight for a sore eyes.

see out of the corner of one's eye *jemanden aus dem Augenwinkel betrachten* **A:** catch a (only) short/ quick glimpse of him/it **B:** I saw Jack last night. Did you give him my regards? – It wasn't possible, I came out of the restaurant and I saw him out of the corner of my eye, as he drove off in a taxi.

in the twinkling of an eye *im Handumdrehen* **A:** in a flash **B:** When Jack learnt his wife had just given birth to twins, he was at the hospital in the twinkling of an eye.

be up to one's eyes in work *bis zum Hals in Arbeit stecken* **V:** up to his eyes in debt, problems etc **A:** be up to one's ears/eyeballs in **B:** Forget about inviting John to the theatre, he's up to his eyes in work this month.

that's one in the eye for someone *Das war für jemanden ein Schlag ins Gesicht* **A:** be a slap in the face for him **B:** He was sure about getting the job at his uncle's company, then he got the letter of refusal, that was one in the eye for him.

There is more in(to) that than meets the eye *Da steckt mehr dahinter* **A:** there's some other reason or something else behind it **B:** The neighbours shortened their holiday, because the weather was so bad. There's more in that than meets the eye, I saw the wife the morning they returned, and her face was covered in bruises.

do something without batting an eyelid *ohne mit der Wimper zu zucken* **V:** without blinking an eyelid **A:** not bat an eyelid **B:** Jack accepted his mother's second marriage with an ex-convict, without batting an eyelid.

not bat an eyelid *nicht mit der Wimper zucken* **V:** not blink an eyelid **A:** do something without batting an eyelid **B:** Many people don't like injections, but as the doctor pushed the needle into

BODY

Susan's vein, she didn't bat an eyelid.

do something with one's eyes shut *etwas mit verbundenen Augen tun* **A:** do something blindfolded, easily **B:** How did Peter, as a lecturer in Philosophy, manage to repair your TV? – Before studying, he spent 10 years in an electrical firm, he repaired it with his eyes shut.

drive off right before one's eyes *jemandem vor der Nase wegfahren* **A:** drive off/ in front of my very eyes or under my very nose **B:** That stupid bus drove off this morning right before my eyes, otherwise I would have been at work on time.

FACE

stand face to face *Auge in Auge gegenüberstehen* **A:** face each other **B:** As the protest marchers reached the atomic power station, the police and demonstrators were standing face to face.

face the facts *den Tatsachen ins Auge sehen* **A:** look the facts in your eye **B:** New investments are out of the question, with our decreasing profits we have to face the facts and reduce all unnecessary costs.

see by someone's face *etwas an jemandes Nasenspitze erkennen* **V:** tell by one's face. **A:** see it in his eyes **B:** As the old lady told us she had found a large box of diamonds in her garden, we could see by her face that she wasn't telling the truth.

beam all over one's face *über beide Ohren grinsen* **V:** grin all over his face **A:** grin like a cheshire cat **B:** We knew our son had passed the exam, he came out of school beaming all over his face.

Let's face it *Sehen wir den Tatsachen ins Auge* **A:** let's be honest about it **B:** Let's face it, the whole morning we've looked at possibilities to save the company, but our debts are too high; we'll have to close down the company.

be a slap in the face for someone *ein Schlag ins Gesicht für jemanden sein* **A:** be a set-back **B:** They had been close friends for a year, and when she didn't invite him to her birthday, that was a slap in the face for him.

Face

make/pull a long face *ein langes Gesicht machen* **A:** pull a long face **B:** Making a long face like that won't help you, I can't pay you back until the end of the month. He didn't get the job and left the interview pulling a long face.

lose (one's) face *sein Gesicht verlieren* **A:** go down a peg or two **B:** The boss knows he's made the wrong decision, but it's useless telling him, he would never admit it and lose (his) face.

save one's face *sein Gesicht wahren* **A:** get out of that one **B:** He wanted to snatch the old lady's hand-bag, but saw the police approaching, and saved his face by helping the lady across the road.

can't look someone in the face *jemandem nicht ins Gesicht schauen können* **A:** can't/won't directly confront someone **B:** After having an affair with my neighbour's wife, I couldn't look him in the face for weeks.

laugh in someone's face *jemandem ins Gesicht lachen* **A:** mock or redicule someone **B:** After their argument the evening before, John told her he was divorcing her, and she just laughed in his face.

lie to someone's face *jemandem ins Gesicht lügen* **V:** (more emphatic) lie straight/right to my face **A:** lie openly in front of someone **B:** My boss promised me promotion 2 months ago, and suddenly told me yesterday that I needed more experience, he lied to my face, he's given the position to his nephew.

say something to one's face *jemandem etwas ins Gesicht sagen* **A:** tell someone something directly/personally **B:** If the trainer doesn't think I'm good enough for the team, then he shouldn't tell others behind my back, but say it (straight/right) to my face.

keep a straight face *keine Miene verziehen* **A:** remain serious **B:** When our daughter was trying to convince us that the first moon-landing took place in an American film studio, we kept a straight face until she went to the disco.

BODY

be written all over one's face *jemandem steht etwas ins Gesicht geschrieben* **A:** see/read something in one's face **B:** Jack said he was fit for the football game, but it was written all over his face, that he was feeling very ill.

fall flat on one's face *auf die Nase fallen* **A:** come a cropper **B:** Jack loved reading and opened a book shop, but had no idea of business; he fell flat on his face after 6 months when his shop went bankrupt.

shut the door in someone's face *jemandem die Tür vor der Nase zuschlagen* **V:** (stronger) slam the door in someone's face **A:** close the door in his face **B:** After the hefty argument, his wife left the room and shut the door in his face.

face up to something *sich einer Sache stellen, den Tatsachen ins Auge sehen* **A:** come to terms with **B:** Darling, you have to stop buying so many clothes, and face up to the fact, that we haven't got the money until I get my new job.

show one's face *sich sehen lassen, auftauchen* **A:** appear, come on the scene **B:** Tommy is hiding somewhere in the garden, don't worry he'll show his face when he smells dinner.

stare someone in the face *jemandem entgegen starren* **A:** look at him (in the face) **B:** Peter should sell his company while he still can, bankruptcy has been staring him in the face for months.

be two-faced *doppelzüngig sein* **A:** be double-faced **B:** At the exhibition, Jack told me he adored my paintings – Then you obviously didn't know he's two-faced, at my party he was saying he'd never seen so much rubbish in his life.

take someone at face value *jemandem blind vertrauen* **A:** believe someone blindly **B:** I got lost and a man stopped, saying he knew the way and I should drive behind him; we got lost again, if I hadn't have taken him at face value, I wouldn't have been so late.

FOOT/FEET

put one's foot in it *ins Fettnäpfchen treten* **A:** say the wrong thing there **B:** You put your foot in it (there) by telling John how wonderful his wife is, they divorced last year.

have one foot in the grave *mit einem Fuß im Grabe stehen* **A:** be on the point of dying **B:** His lung cancer has unfortunately spread to his liver, I fear he already has one foot in the grave.

put one's foot down *jemandem zeigen, wo es langgeht, ein Machtwort sprechen* **A:** impose one's authority **B:** His sixteen-year-old daughter had started coming home at 3 or 4 in the morning, then her father put his foot down, and told her school girls should be back at midnight at the latest.

foot the bill *die Rechnung bezahlen* **A:** pay/settle the bill **B:** Jack was worried about paying for the expensive meal with his new girl friend, when fortunately her father joined them and said he'd foot the bill.

catch someone on the wrong foot *jemanden auf dem falschen Fuß erwischen* **A:** catch someone unaware or in a precarious situation **B:** I wanted to congratulate Jack and his wife to their 25th anniversary, but caught Jack on the wrong foot – he was flirting with a girl in his car as I went to their door with flowers.

start on the wrong foot *einen schlechten Start haben* **A:** begin something the wrong way **B:** Well you certainly started on the wrong foot by asking your boss for a holiday, you've only been with company for a month!

gain a (firm) foothold *(festen) Fuß fassen* **A:** get a firm footing, basis **B:** After the allies had taken Baghdad, it looked as if they had gained a firm foothold in Iraq.

follow in his footsteps *in jemandes Fußstapfen treten* **V:** follow in someone's tracks **A:** follow someone's example **B:** George is following in his father's footsteps. His father is a judge and George has just started studying law.

BODY

be back on one's feet again *wieder auf den Beinen sein* **A:** be fighting fit again, recover from an illness **B:** I haven't seen Peter since his football injury last month. – Don't worry, he's back on his feet again, and already training with the team.

be on one's feet (for a long time) *(ständig) auf den Beinen sein* **A:** be (always) on the go **B:** The young medical students must be exhausted, they have been on their feet for the last 24 hours in the hospital.

have/get cold feet *kalte Füße bekommen/haben* **A:** chicken out (of something) **B:** My bank has suddenly refused to give that big loan they promised me. – Well, I expect they heard that your company was in difficulties, and now they have cold feet.

always fall on one's feet *immer auf die Füße fallen* **A:** land on one's own two feet, (always) land on all fours **B:** He was fired from his company last week, and yesterday he got a better job at twice the salary; typical, he always falls on his feet.

cut the ground from under one's feet *jemandem den Boden unter den Füßen wegziehen* **A:** endanger one's livelihood **B:** With the increase in large supermarkets the small retailers have had the ground cut from under their feet.

have both feet (firmly) on the ground *mit beiden Beinen (fest) auf dem Boden stehen* **V:** have both feet firmly planted on the ground **A:** be safe/sure as a rock **B:** George has been accused of transferring money from his company to a private account. – I can't believe that, George has always had both feet (firmly) on the ground.

walk one's feet off *sich die Hacken ablaufen (nach etwas), sich die Hacken abrennen* **V:** walk himself off his feet/legs **A:** walk till he drops/dropped **B:** John walked his feet off looking for the hospital in the Spanish village, then he was told it was in the next town, and took a taxi.

stand on one's own (two) feet *auf eigenen Beinen stehen* **A:** be independent, self-assured **B:** Our basic task, as parents, is to allow our children to develop with principles and responsibility, and provide them with an education, so that they can later stand on their own two feet.

sweep/knock someone off one's feet *jemanden von den Socken reißen* **A:** give him wobbly feet **B:** I always thought he was a confirmed bachelor, but when David met the new attractive secretary, she swept him off his feet.

find one's feet *sich zurechtfinden* **A:** come to terms with the new/difficult situation **B:** Didn't your son have problems changing schools at the age of 8? – Thankfully not, he soon found his feet, and has made a lot of friends.

FINGER

lay a finger on someone *jemanden anfassen, Hand anlegen* **V:** (not) lay a hand on someone **A:** get anywhere near someone **B:** If you lay a finger on my baby, then I'll call the police.

not put one's finger on it *sich nicht genau an etwas erinnern* **A:** not pull something together **B:** I can't put my finger on it at the moment, but Jack said something yesterday which sounded as if the company was in deep trouble.

twist someone round one's little finger *jemanden um den (kleinen) Finger wickeln* **A:** put someone where you want **B:** Jack didn't want to go on an expensive holiday, but his wife was able to twist him round her little finger, and they went.

not lift/move/stir a finger *keinen Finger rühren/krumm machen* **A:** not help a single bit **B:** Lazy John went to the cinema, and didn't lift a finger as his parents renovated his flat.

pull/get one's finger out *Nägel mit Köpfen machen, Ärmel hochkrempeln* **A:** pull one's socks up **B:** If you want to pass your final exam, then you've got to pull your finger out, and not sit in front of the computer playing games.

put one's finger on it *den Nagel auf den Kopf treffen* **A:** hit the hammer on the nail **B:** You've put your finger on it, why George isn't studying for his exams – too many late night parties.

BODY

keep one's fingers crossed (for someone) *jemandem die Daumen drücken* **V:** cross one's fingers (for someone) **A:** wish you good luck **B:** I'm sure you'll pass your driving test, but I'll keep my fingers crossed for you.

(let) something slip through one's fingers *sich etwas durch die Lappen gehen lassen* **A:** just miss a good chance/opportunity **B:** I let that sports car slip through my fingers, if I'd decided more quickly, the car would have been mine last week.

work one's fingers to the bone *sich die Finger wund arbeiten* **A:** work his nose to the grindstone **B:** When his wife lost her job and his 27 year old daughter wanted to study, he had to work his fingers to the bone to get the extra money.

(can) count it on the fingers of one hand *etwas an einer Hand abzählen (können)* **V:** (short version) can count that on one hand **B:** Your mother has never liked travelling, how often has she been abroad? – I can count that on the fingers of one hand!

FINGERTIPS

be something to one's fingertips *etwas durch und durch sein* **V:** down to one's fingertips **A:** from head to foot **B:** I wouldn't start discussions on socialism with Peter, he's a conservative to his fingertips.

GALL

have the gall to do something *die Frechheit haben, etwas zu tun* **A:** have the impudence or audacity to do it **B:** Jack was fired after the super market manager found him stealing money, then he had the gall to ask for his job back after a week.

GUTS

have the guts to do something *den Mut haben, etwas zu tun* **A:** have the courage/strength/ nerve **B:** He's got the guts to start that job in the prison, but it's not really the right thing for him, he'll be depressed after a few months.

HAIR

not touch a hair on one's head *jemandem kein Haar krümmen* **V:** not harm a hair on his head/ body **A:** would not hurt a fly **B:** I'm unsure about leaving

Hand

our son with your brother, he got divorced 6 months ago. Darling, he wouldn't touch a hair on his head, he left his wife, because she didn't want any children.

make one's hair stand on end *jemandem stehen die Haare zu Berge* **A:** make one's hair curl **B:** Jack never believed in ghosts, but on a holiday in a Scottish castle he was woken by the noise of dragging chains, and it made his hair stand on end.

split hairs *Haarspalterei betreiben* **V:** That's hair-splitting **A:** argue about nothing or over petty things **B:** I refuse to go on the train, the bus is 20 cents cheaper and is 5 minutes quicker. – You're splitting hairs, the station is nearer and we've just missed the last bus anyway.

HAND

don't bite the hand that feeds you *Man soll die Hand nicht beißen, die einen füttert* **A:** (generally negative form) don't endanger one's very existence **B:** I wouldn't bite the hand that feeds you, by always insulting your parents – they've sacrificed a lot to financially support your studies.

try one's hand at something *etwas ausprobieren, versuchen* **A:** try something out **B:** Your writing skills are not very good, why don't you try your hand at painting.

give someone a big hand *jemandem großen Beifall spenden* **A:** give someone a big applause **B:** When Jack comes into the office, we'll give him a big hand; if he hadn't seen the flames in the cellar last night, our office building wouldn't have been here this morning.

be an old hand at *ein alter Hase in etwas sein* **A:** be experienced/competent at a particular thing **B:** No need to worry, we can go on holiday and leave my father to control the painters, he's an old hand at house decoration and repairs.

be hand in glove with someone *mit jemandem unter einer Decke stecken* **V:** work h. in g. with **A:** conspire/work (illegally) together **B:** The police arrested George as he robbed the bank, but

BODY

knew he was hand in glove with his brother, who was waiting in a car round the corner.

force someone's hand *jemanden unter Druck setzen* **A:** change someone's opinion/attitude through pressure **B:** Why did you lend Jack your new sport's car, you don't allow anyone to drive it. – He must have forced your hand, he knows you want to go out with his sister.

be (close/near) at hand *zur Hand sein, in Reichweite sein* **V:** be at hand **A:** be within easy reach **B:** We're your neighbours, so while your parents are in hospital, if you need help, we're always close at hand.

get it at first/second hand *etwas aus erster/zweiter Hand hören* **A:** receive/hear something from the original source (at first hand) or from another person (at second hand) **B:** The driver who overtook the tractor and hit the on-coming car was to blame, I got the details at first hand, I spoke to the tractor driver.

give someone a free hand *jemandem freie Hand lassen* **A:** give someone complete freedom to do **B:** We got divorced when our children were 4 and 3 years of age, but my ex-husband gave me a free hand in bringing the children up.

have a hand in something *(bei etwas) die Hand im Spiel haben* **A:** play/have a part in something **B:** Jack told me he built the garden shed alone. I don't believe that, I'm sure his father had a hand in it.

live from hand to mouth *von/aus der Hand in den Mund leben* **A:** barely survive **B:** In the first years after the war, when food and work were almost non-existent, many people had to live from hand to mouth.

be one's right hand *jemandes rechte Hand sein* **V:** be one's right-hand man **B:** When the director gave me that youngster as my assistant I was very sceptical, but after 6 months he's become my right hand.

give/lend someone a hand with *jemandem zur Hand gehen* **A:** help someone out **B:** Give us a hand George, we can't carry

Hand

this table into the house by ourselves. Can you give me a hand with my homework, I didn't understand anything the teacher said.

eat out of someone's hand *jemandem aus der Hand fressen* **V:** have someone eating out of one's hand **A:** be in the palm of his hand **B:** We shouldn't have left Tom with your mother for the weekend, he's been misbehaving all week. Don't worry, she'll spoil him as she always does and he'll soon be eating out of her hand.

raise one's hand to/at someone *die Hand gegen jemanden erheben* **V:** lift one's hands at/to someone **A:** about to hit/threaten someone (by lifting one's hand) **B:** Don't you raise your hand to me, young lad, otherwise I'll stop your pocket money next week as well.

do at the turn of a hand *im Handumdrehen* **A:** in a flash/jiffy **B:** When Fred's car skidded on an icy patch, he had his car under control at the turn of a hand.

have/gain the upper hand *die Oberhand haben/gewinnen* **V:** have the whip hand **A:** have the stronger position **B:** Before they married John had the upper hand, but after 6 months of married life his wife had gained the upper hand.

be a great hand (at) *sehr große Hilfe sein* **V:** a big hand **A:** be a great help/assistence (iron: then the exact opposite = be no help at all) **B:** Thanks for helping me moving the furniture, you were a great hand. Jack is a great hand at giving advice, but when it comes to doing it, he's useless.

get out of hand *außer Kontrolle geraten* **A:** be/get out of control **B:** When the teacher had to leave the pupils alone for 10 minutes, the class got out of hand and started throwing books at each other.

(must) hand it to someone *Das muss man ihm lassen* **A:** must acknowledge/credit someone for what he's done **B:** A pity you were only third in the sailing tournament, but I've got to hand it to you, your sailing in that bad weather was brilliant.

BODY

throw in one's hand *aufgeben, das Spiel verloren geben* **A:** throw in one's cards **B:** Before the last game of the chess contest, he realised he didn't have a chance, and threw in his hand.

make/be a poor hand at *ungeschickt/unfähig sein* **A:** not be cut out for **B:** I'd make a poor hand at helping you paint your garden fence, more paint would end up on the lawn than on the fence.

know it/someone like the back of one's hand *etwas wie seine Westentasche kennen, in und auswendig kennen* **V:** like the palm of one's hand **A:** know someone inside out **B:** Do you think Jack will find the street where the party is? – No problem, he spent his youth in the village and knows it like the back of his hand.

keep a tight hand on someone *streng im Zaum halten* **V:** keep a tight reign on someone **A:** keep someone under strict control/surveillance **B:** When your son left hospital after his knee operation, he was operated again 2 weeks later after a football match. You should have kept a tight hand on him for the first months.

come away empty-handed *mit leeren Händen ausgehen* **V:** return or come back empty-handed **A:** come away penniless **B:** Jack was hoping to win at least the bronze medal in the Olympic games, but came away empty-handed.

take someone/something off one's hands *ihm jemanden/etwas abnehmen* **A:** give somone a break from something **B:** I've been looking after my 8 year old nephew this week, could you take him off my hands on Saturday afternoon so I can go to the football match?

be caught with one's hands in the till *auf frischer Tat ertappt werden* **A:** (for any criminal offence) be caught stealing, pinching **B:** After working 4 years in the supermarket, Susan needed money and made a silly mistake and was caught with her hands in the till.

have one's hands full *alle Hände voll zu tun haben* **A:** not have a

Hand

minute to breathe **B:** I can't play golf with you today, I've got my hands full, I'm looking after the baby while my wife is in hospital and the plumber is coming to mend the pipe.

be/lie in one's hands *Es liegt in jemandes Hand* **A:** something is up to you now **B:** I've helped you with the theoretical exams, but the final practical test in flying is in your hands now.

dirty one's hands *sich die Hände schmutzig machen* **V:** soil one's hands **A:** get involved in something dirty/illegal **B:** I wouldn't dirty your hands (by) doing business with that firm, they are illegally importing drugs and weapons.

have only one pair of hands *nur zwei Hände haben* **A:** can't do it all (alone) **B:** I can't look after the children and cook the dinner, I've only (got) one pair of hands.

play (right) into someone's hands *jemandem in die Hände spielen* **V:** (among two persons) play into each other's hands **B:** You shouldn't have told your competitors your company is in debt, they want to buy your company, you played right into their hands.

have one's hands tied *jemandem sind die Hände gebunden* **V:** my hands are tied. **A:** not be free to act as one would like **B:** Sorry, I can't lend you the company van again, my boss promoted me to head of the transport department, so I have my hands tied more than before.

lay (one's) hands on someone *jemanden schlagen* **A:** hit or attack someone **B:** If you lay hands on me, I'll call the police.

take one's life in one's hands *sein Leben aufs Spiel setzen* **A:** put one's life at great risk **B:** Don't let George drive you to the airport, you'll be taking your life in your hands, he got his licence only last week and has caused 3 accidents already.

win something (with one's) hands down *spielend/ohne Mühe/mit links gewinnen* **A:** win (sport, contest, game etc) with my eyes shut **B:** His opponent had been ill three weeks and

BODY

was unable to train, Jack won the race hands down.

HEAD

be soft in the head *eine weiche Birne haben* **V:** be weak in the head **A:** be thick/dense/stupid **B:** I don't think Jack could help you prepare for your school exam in mathematics, he's soft in the head.

put ideas into someone's head *jemanden auf dumme Gedanken bringen* **A:** put weird/strange or funny ideas into someone's head **B:** Dad, I'd like a car for my birthday! – Have your student friends been putting ideas into your head again, you know we haven't got the money!

be head over heels in love *bis über beide Ohren verliebt sein* **A:** fall for someone completely **B:** We'll have to ring Peter, we need him in the team for the match on Saturday, forget him, he's head over heels in love.

come/bring to a head *den Höhepunkt erreichen, sich zuspitzen* **A:** reach boiling-point **B:** The hefty disagreement among the party leaders has come to a head, the foreign minister was asked to resign. The minister brought the scandal to a head by resigning from the government.

not make head or tail of it *aus etwas nicht schlau werden* **A:** be baffled **B:** I've read the instructions for our new video recorder twice, and I still can't make head or tail of it, we'll have ring your brother, he's an expert on electronics.

go to one's head *etwas steigt jemandem zu Kopf* **A:** get/become a little conceited **B:** John's passed his theoretical exam at the pilot school with excellent marks, I hope it doesn't go to his head, because the practical flying test is far more difficult.

keep one's head (on) *einen kühlen Kopf bewahren* **A:** keep cool **B:** As the Christmas tree suddenly went into flames, she kept her head, and put a blanket over the tree and stopped the fire.

lose one's head *den Kopf verlieren* **A:** get excited **B:** After his team was 2 goals ahead, the opponents got two goals through

Head

penalties and when his team made an own goal, the trainer lost his head.

put something into one's head *sich etwas in den Kopf setzen* **A:** set/put one's mind to something **B:** After 4 years as a stewardess, she put it into her head to become a pilot, and in spite of her age and entering a male dominated profession, she finished the training course.

put something out of one's head *sich etwas aus dem Kopf schlagen* **A:** dismiss it from one' mind **B:** Put that out of your head, young daughter, wanting to spend 6 weeks in India with a boy-friend is not possible at the age of fourteen.

puzzle one's head over it *sich über etwas den Kopf zerbrechen* **A:** to rack one's brains over something **B:** He's been puzzling his head over his missing car key for days, he should simply order a new one and the problem is solved.

keep running/going through someone's head *jemandem geht etwas nicht mehr aus dem Kopf/Sinn* **A:** keep turning in my thoughts **B:** At the funeral, it kept running through my head how unlucky he was to get cancer at the age of 22.

not get something into one's head *jemandem will etwas nicht in den Kopf gehen* **A:** not grasp/ accept something **B:** She still can't get it into her head that at 75 years of age, she can't drive her car as safely as before.

not get something out of one's head *etwas nicht aus dem Kopf bekommen* **V:** not get it out of one's mind **A:** not (want to) believe or understand something **B:** I can't get it out of my head that she married a man 40 years older than herself.

run your head against a brick wall *mit dem Kopf gegen die Wand rennen* **V:** against a stone wall **B:** I wouldn't force Jack into marrying you, you'll be running your head against a brick wall, he needs time, he lost his wife only 3 months ago.

keep one's head above water *sich mit dem Kopf über Wasser halten* **A:** keep the wolf from the door **B:** After losing his job, he kept his head above water by stopping smoking and reducing his telephone bill.

turn someone's head 1) *etwas steigt jemandem zu Kopf* **A:** go to one's head **B:** John's election to Presidency of our debating society has turned his head, he only talks to his vice president and treasurer, and virtually ignores the other club members.

turn someone's head 2) *jemandem den Kopf verdrehen* **A:** infatuate someone **B:** The new attractive secretary turned the boss's head on first encounter, he was confused for the rest of the day.

laugh one's head off *sich totlachen* **A:** laugh oneself silly **B:** My mother is normally very reserved, but the theatre comedy was so good, she laughed her head off during the whole performance.

be head and shoulders above someone *jemandem haushoch überlegen sein* **V:** be head and shoulders better than him **A:** be miles apart from someone **B:** You needn't apply for the position of group head, the director has found a person who's head and shoulders above you, my friend.

have one's head in the clouds. *über den Wolken schweben* **A:** be in a daydream/dreamworld **B:** You must have your head in the clouds, darling, we'll never pull the money together to buy such a house.

be at loggerheads *sich in den Haaren liegen* **A:** be in a continual dispute or argument with **B:** Have Jack's divorce proceedings been settled? – No, his lawyer and his wife's lawyer are still at loggerheads on the question of maintenance.

make headway *vorwärts kommen* **A:** make progress **B:** In spite of the strong current and storm, the sailors were making headway, and expected to reach their destination only 2 hours later than planned.

HEART

learn (off) by heart *auswendig lernen* **A:** learn from memory **B:** Jack got the best marks in the Chemistry exam, but he doesn't

Heart

understand a thing about the subject, he just learnt the answers off by heart.

have a heart of gold *ein goldenes Herz haben, gutherzig sein* **A:** be an angel/treasure **B:** Apart from her occasional angry outbursts, she has a heart of gold and helps everyone.

one's heart is (not) in it *(nicht) mit dem Herzen bei etwas sein* **A:** put everything into it **B:** Before his father died, George was the most enthusiastic accountant in the firm, but he now makes mistakes, and hasn't got his heart in his work any more.

have one's heart in the right place *das Herz am rechten Fleck haben* **A:** be a good person in his heart **B:** With his shouting and criticising, you might think he has a bad character, but he has his heart in the right place, when it comes to helping people.

set one's heart on something *sein Herz an etwas/jemanden hängen* **A:** want something above all else **B:** Jack has certainly set his heart on spending 6 weeks touring round America, he even sold his beloved sports car to pay for the holiday.

take something to heart *sich etwas zu Herzen nehmen/zu Herzen gehen lassen* **A:** take something too seriously or badly **B:** The Doctor only told you to watch your weight because of health reasons, darling, don't take it to heart, you're certainly not fat.

have a heart of stone *ein Herz aus Stein haben* **A:** be cold as ice **B:** When he hit the woman pushing her pram on the zebra crossing, he checked his car and drove off, he must have a heart of stone.

not have the heart to do something *es nicht über das Herz bringen, etwas zu tun* **A:** not find it in one's heart to **B:** When our daughter's bay rabbit died while she was holiday, we didn't have the heart to tell her, and bought a similar rabbit before she returned.

be the heart of the matter *der Kern der Sache* **A:** be the essential point **B:** They're getting divorced after only 6 months, they have totally different poli-

BODY

tical views. Well, the heart of the matter is – her husband loves someone else, and was forced into the marriage by his mother.

lose heart *den Mut verlieren* **A:** give up, lose courage **B:** There are good and bad teachers, and you've been unlucky, but don't lose heart, keep to your final goal and I'm sure you'll pass your final exam.

Have a heart! *Sei nett!/Gib deinem Herzen einen Stoß* **A:** Be reasonable! **B:** Your husband already has a second job in the evening, and now you want him to do a delivery job starting at 3 a.m. in the morning. Have a heart!

put one's heart (and soul) into something *sich mit Leib und Seele einer Sache widmen* **A:** put everything into it **B:** A pilot's job also has its routine, stuck in a small place, worrying about the weather all the time. If you can't put your heart into the job, then you should choose another career.

do to one's heart's content *etwas nach Herzenslust tun* **A:** do it as long as one likes **B:** The neighbours are on holiday for a fortnight, you can practice playing your trumpet to your heart's content.

HEELS

tread (hard) on the heels of someone *jemandem (dicht) auf den Fersen sein* **A:** follow closely on the heels of someone **B:** After the 11th of September, the Americans have been treading on the heels of everyone suspected of terrorism.

LAP

live in the lap of luxury *wie Gott in Frankreich leben* **A:** live like a king **B:** After 5 years imprisonment in Russia, he finally returned to his home and family, it seemed to him that he was living in the lap of luxury.

LEG

pull someone's leg *jemanden auf dem Arm nehmen* **A:** make a fool of someone **B:** Jack, the boss wants to speak to you about promotion and an increased salary immediately! – Come on, I know he's still on holiday as well, stop pulling my leg!

talk the hind leg off a donkey. *jemanden zutexten, voll reden* **A:** talk non-stop **B:** Joan has invited me for meal and a discussion on religion. Enjoy the meal, mate, but the discussion will be hard, she can talk the hind leg off a donkey.

stretch one's legs *sich die Beine vertreten, spazieren gehen* **A:** excercise one's legs **B:** After sitting 3 hours in the theatre, I'm looking forward to stretching my legs, shall we walk round the park?

be on one's/its last legs *aus dem letzten Loch pfeifen* **A:** be on one's last tether **B:** We ought to stop at the next hotel, James, after 15 miles non-stop walking, you're on your last legs.

give someone a leg-up *jemandem (nach oben) helfen* **A:** help someone **B:** When I first started with the company, John gave me a leg-up by introducing me to the directors and board members.

LIP

keep a stiff upper lip *die Ohren steif halten* **A:** keep in fighting **B:** The boss wants to dismiss me, for visiting my wife at the hospital too often. – Keep a stiff upper lip, he'll change his opinion, his wife had a bad car accident this morning.

pay lip service *Lippenbekenntnis ablegen* **B:** After the lecture on communism Jack spent an hour talking enthusiastically with the lecturer. Has he changed his political views then? – No, Jack was just paying lip service, he's a devote capitalist.

MOUTH

have a big mouth *eine große Klappe haben* **A:** be a loud mouth **B:** Jack has always had a big mouth when it came to his football ability. Since he's playing in the first team on Saturday, he can show us what he can really do.

shut your mouth *Halt den Mund* **V:** shut your trap, kisser (mostly by children = gob, cake-hole) **A:** shut up **B:** You've been shouting about the club's bad policies for 20 minutes, can't you shut your mouth and let the other members give their opinions?

BODY

make one's mouth water *jemandem läuft das Wasser im Mund zusammen* **A:** one's mouth is watering **B:** Dinner will soon be ready, when you see what a delicious meal mummy has cooked, it will make your mouth water.

by word of mouth *von Mund zu Mund* **B:** That new product is so good, you've no need to advertise, the news will be quickly passed around by word of mouth.

put words into his mouth *jemandem die Worte in den Mund legen* **B:** When the police told the youngster he was at the disco when the fight started, he responded. – You're putting words into my mouth, I said I was in bed ill that evening.

take the words out of his mouth *jemandem das Wort aus dem Mund nehmen* **A:** beat someone to it **B:** John, that's the worst film I've ever seen! You've taken the words out of my mouth, I wanted to suggest we only go to the theatre in future.

leave a nasty taste in the mouth *einen bitteren Nachgeschmack hinterlassen* **A:** leave an unpleasant/bad feeling/impression with someone **B:** So your girl friend has left you. – Yes, I'm not too sad, but when she told me I'm incapable of having a stable relationship with anyone, that left a nasty taste in the (my) mouth.

straight from the horse's mouth *aus erster Hand* **A:** get/receive it at/from first hand **B:** Jack was never involved in that bank robbery, was he? – Yes, he was identified, I got it straight from the horse's mouth, I met the manager of the bank today.

melt in one's mouth *sich etwas auf der Zunge zergehen lassen* **A:** go down like a treat **B:** When he told his father he had won a scholarship as best student, the word „best" melted in his mouth.

MUSCLE

not move a muscle *sich nicht rühren* **A:** not move/budge an inch, Nuance 2: be lazy, not help **B:** The guards outside Buckingham Palace have to stand there for hours without moving a muscle.

NECK

break one's neck *sich (beinah, fast) das Genick brechen, sich fast überschlagen* **A:** (nearly, almost) kill onself **B:** I nearly broke my neck driving to the station to collect you on time, you could have told me you'd taken a later train.

stick one's neck out *seinen Hals riskieren* **A:** risk one's neck **B:** As a very weak swimmer, Jack stuck his neck out and jumped into the stormy sea to save the baby.

be a pain in the neck *eine Nervensäge sein* **A:** be/become a burden or (bloody) nuisance **B:** Ringing us everyday with problems about booking your holiday doesn't interest us; you're a pain in the neck, we've got our own problems.

hang round someone's neck *jemanden am Hals haben* **V:** have someone/something (hanging) round one's neck **A:** stick round someone **B:** Are you mad, John, I know your mother-in-law very well, if you invite her for the weekend, she'll be hanging round our necks for months.

be up to one's neck in something *bis zum Hals in etwas (z. B. Schwierigkeiten) stecken* **A:** be stuck in it up to one's ears **B:** If the police catch us, you can't argue you had nothing to do with the robbery; you drove us to the bank – you're up to your neck in it, as we are.

neck and neck *Kopf an Kopf* **A:** absolutely level **B:** The Canadian and British 100 metre runners appeared to cross the finishing line neck and neck, but the camera showed the Canadian had won.

breathe down someone's neck *über jemandes Schulter schauen* **V:** (generally negative) stop breathing/don't breathe **A:** peer over someone's shoulder **B:** If you want me to mend your broken necklace, darling, then stop breathing down my neck, I can't concentrate.

NERVE

lose one's nerve *die Nerven verlieren/den Mut verlieren* **A:** lose one's courage **B:** When the boxer heard of his opponent chosen for his next championship fight, he lost his nerve and postponed the fight due to illness.

BODY

have the nerve to do *die Unverschämtheit haben (etwas zu tun)* **A:** have the impudence **B:** After borrowing our garden watering can, our neighbour had the nerve to use our lawn mower without asking us.

be a bundle of nerves *ein Nervenbündel sein* **V:** be a bag of nerves **A:** be a nervous wreck **B:** When Pamela was attacked on her way home in the dark park, she was a bundle of nerves for days, and vowed she'd take a taxi, if she ever missed the last bus again.

get on someone's nerves *jemandem auf die Nerven/den Wecker gehen* **A:** get on one's wick (used by women: get on my tits) **B:** Jack is an arrogant know-all, he gets on my nerves, when he starts preaching that he knows better than everybody else.

NOSE

can't see beyond the end of one's nose *man kann die Hand nicht vor Augen sehen* **A:** can't see a thing in front of me **B:** I'll have to go into first gear and drive like a snail in this fog, I can't see beyond the end of my nose.

turn up one's nose at something *über etwas die Nase rümpfen* **A:** look down one's nose **B:** She turned up her nose at Jack's suggestion on going to Brighton for a holiday. Nothing but the Riviera is good enough for her.

stick one's nose in(to) everything *in alles seine Nase stecken* **V:** poke his nose into everything (or everywhere) **B:** Our neighbour retired last year, and knows about every incident, news or scandal in our village – he sticks his nose in(to) everything.

snatch something from (right) under one's nose *jemandem etwas vor der Nase wegschnappen* **V:** from under his very nose. **A:** snatch it before/in front of my (very) eyes **B:** That's unfair, Granny promised me the last piece of cake, and you've snatched it from right under my nose.

have a (good) nose for something *den richtigen Riecher für etwas haben* **A:** have a keen sense or good feeling for something **B:** The art director chose pictures, which appealed to the majority of the public, he certainly had a (good) nose for

Nose

their interests, his exhibition was a success.

just follow one's nose *immer der Nase nach* **A:** go/ drive straight ahead **B:** Turn first left at the petrol station, and then just follow your nose until you come to the Registry office.

look down one's nose (at someone) *die Nase rümpfen* **A:** show one's disapproval or distaste **B:** He looked down his nose, when he saw the new bank trainee enter the office in jeans and jogging shoes.

push it under one's nose *jemanden mit der Nase auf etwas stoßen* **A:** rub his nose in it **B:** Kids, we're arriving at the border and the custom's officer looks angry, and the car boot is full of wine, so don't push it under his nose by staring at the back of the car.

thumb your nose at someone *jemandem eine (lange) Nase zeigen* **A:** pull one's nose at someone **B:** Don't thumb your nose at me, friend. You may have won the first round, but the winner of the tournament is decided after three golf rounds, and I'm just warming up.

under someone's (very) nose *(direkt) vor seinen Augen* **A:** right/directly in front of you **B:** In our new house, the public swimming pool is under our very nose, I'll be swimming every day.

lead someone by the nose *jemanden an der Nase herumführen* **A:** lead someone on a wild goose chase **B:** The murderer led the police by the nose for 3 months, then they finally caught him, going into a man's toilet dressed as a woman.

poke one's nose into something *seine Nase in etwas hineinstecken* **A:** nose around in some/ everything **B:** He's been poking his nose into my private affairs again. After my father's firm went bankrupt, the tax inspectors were nosing around in his documents for days.

rub one's nose in it *jemandem etwas unter die Nase reiben* **A:** (short): rub it in **B:** It was bad enough for poor Jack, unluckily losing all that money – there's no need to rub his nose it in, by reminding him all the time.

BODY

keep one's nose clean *sauber bleiben* **A:** keep out of trouble **B:** The police have caught you stealing money from old people again, if you don't want your wife to leave you, then keep your nose clean from now on.

pay through the nose *tief in die Tasche greifen* **A:** dig deep into his purse **B:** The reduced offers for the new computers finished last week, I had to pay through the nose for the one I bought today.

be nosy/a nosey parker *neugierig/ein Topfgucker sein* **A:** inquisitive **B:** Darling, why do you want to go shopping by yourself? – Don't be so nosy, it's your birthday next Saturday.

PALM

have someone in the palm of one's hand *jemanden fest in der Hand haben* **A:** have someone under one's control/influence **B:** Jack had a very strong character, but since his marriage, his wife has him in the palm of her hand, he does everything she tells him.

SHOULDER

shoulder the blame *die Schuld auf sich nehmen* **A:** carry/take the blame on his shoulders **B:** During his holiday his staff didn't finish the report on time, but he shouldered the blame, and told the boss he should have given clearer instructions to his staff.

give someone the cold shoulder *jemandem die kalte Schulter zeigen* **A:** cut someone off **B:** What's up with your girl-friend, she passed us just then and ignored you? – She gave me the cold shoulder, because I told her last night I have another girlfriend.

have a shoulder to cry on *jemanden zum Anlehnen* haben **A:** have someone to console/comfort you **B:** After her parents were killed in a car crash, she was happy to have her Grandmother as a shoulder to cry on.

SKIN

be all skin and bones *nur noch Haut und Knochen sein* **V:** be nothing but skin and bones **A:** be as thin as a rake **B:** Your wife shouldn't have done that diet for 6 months, she's all skin and bones.

jump out of one's skin *sich zu Tode erschrecken* **A:** have of the shock of one's life **B:** The old lady jumped out of her skin, when she opened her house door and saw a burglar searching her cupboards.

save someone's/one's own skin *jemandes/die eigene Haut retten* **A:** save one's/someone's life **B:** She saved her boyfriend Jack's skin, by lying to the police, saying he had spent the whole day with her during the bank robbery.

not (like to) be in someone else's skin *nicht in jemandes Haut stecken mögen* **A:** not like to be in someone else's shoes **B:** You were so drunk flirting with that young girl at the party, that you didn't notice your wife left suddenly. I wouldn't be in your skin when you go home tonight.

get under one's skin *1) jemandem auf die Nerven gehen 2) jemandem unter die Haut gehen* **A:** 1) irritate/annoy 2) touch one (with sentiment or feeling) **B:** 1) You get under my skin with your constant moaning, accept it now and shut up! 2) When my father's coffin was lowered into the earth, it really got under my skin.

by the skin of one's teeth *mit Hängen und Würgen* **A:** in the nick of time **B:** As his brothers were playing with air guns, John put his head out the window and a bullet went into his eyebrow, missing his eye by the skin of his teeth.

have/get a thick skin *ein dickes Fell haben* **V:** be (very) thick-skinned **A:** be insensitive **B:** She won't get upset, if you tell her she's too fat, she's thick-skinned enough to laugh it off.

STOMACH

have no stomach for *nicht den Mumm zu etwas haben* **A:** can't stand it **B:** Peter could never be a surgeon, he's got no stomach for blood.

turn one's stomach *etwas dreht jemandem den Magen um* **A:** make someone sick **B:** All these killings and wars on television really turn my stomach.

BODY

THROAT

words stick in one's throat *jemandem bleiben die Worte im Halse stecken* **A:** couldn't say it for pride, anger etc. **B:** I wanted to congratulate him on getting the first prize in sport, but he had treated my girl friend so badly, that the words stuck in my throat.

have a lump in one's throat *einen Kloß im Hals haben* **A:** say something with an awkward/sad feeling **B:** After my wife's operation, the doctor said there was no chance; when I told my young daughter that mummy would soon be well again, I had a lump in my throat.

be at each other's throats *sich in den Haaren liegen* **A:** be at logger-heads with another **B:** They'll never be close brothers again, since their mother's testament left everything to one of them, they've been at each other's throats.

THUMB

stick out like a sore thumb *etwas springt direkt ins Auge, (Person) auffallen durch Andersartigkeit* **A:** not fit in (with the surroundings) **B:** At the President's party, the consulate's son stuck out like a sore thumb, with bare feet, jeans and hair down to his waist.

thumb a lift *per Anhalter fahren* **A:** get a car driver to stop for you **B:** How did you travel round Italy as a student with little money? – I thumbed a lift from Milan down to Naples and back.

rule of thumb *Faustregel* **V:** do it by rule of thumb = from experience **B:** My wife's cooking is basically rule of thumb, she knows the contents, but not the quantities or how, but gets wonderful results.

have somone under one's thumb *jemanden unter seiner Fuchtel haben* **A:** dominate or control someone **B:** His wife must have him under her thumb, Jack is so polite and helpful at home instead of being loud and rude as he is outside.

twiddle one's thumbs *Däumchen drehen* **A:** have nothing to do **B:** There's no need to sit there twiddling your thumbs till the removal van comes, you can help me pack the books into boxes.

give someone the thumbs up/ down *Daumen nach oben/unten geben* **A:** show a positive/ negative response (success/failure, approval/disapproval, good/ bad news etc) **B:** When I asked Jack whether he had enjoyed the evening with my sister, he smiled politely and gave me the thumbs down.

be all (fingers and) thumbs *zwei linke Hände haben* **V:** his fingers are all thumbs **A:** be clumsy **B:** I wouldn't ask George to sort your stamps according to country and date, he's all (fingers and) thumbs, he'll either lose or damage most of them.

TOE

toe the line *sich an die Regeln halten* **A:** keep in line **B:** You're always late, you disturb all the lessons, if you don't toe the line, young lad, then you'll be expelled from this school.

tread on someone's toes *jemandem auf die Zehen treten* **A:** offend someone **B:** Why did Jack get annoyed when I told his son he should stop playing with that long pointed stick? – Well, he's a very responsible father, I guess he felt you were treading on his toes.

keep someone on his toes *jemanden auf Trab halten* **A:** keep someone alert **B:** The director kept his staff on their toes by giving them new work as soon they were finished with the first job.

TONGUE

hold one's tongue *den Mund halten, sich zurückhalten* **A:** remain silent, Hold your tongue! (= be quiet or shut up!) **B:** He knew which of his class mates had thrown stones at the school windows, but when the police asked him for help, he held his tongue.

lose/find one's tongue *seine Sprache verlieren/wiederfinden* **A:** be speechless/regain one's speech **B:** You're very silent, have you lost your tongue?

keep a civil tongue in your head *etwas in einem netten Ton sagen, höflich bleiben* **A:** speak in a polite way **B:** You mustn't speak to your mother in such a rude

BODY

manner, if you can't keep a civil tongue in your head, then there's no cinema this evening.

be a slip of the tongue *ein Versprecher sein* **A:** twist the words around **B:** When the biology lecturer realised he had been saying orgasm instead organism for the first 5 minutes, he apologised to the students with „Sorry, that was a slip of the tongue."

be on the tip of one's tongue *etwas liegt jemandem auf der Zunge* **A:** try to remember something (generally a word or name) **B:** When the geography teacher asked Tom what the capital (city) of France is, Tom said, it's on the tip of my tongue, and after 5 seconds he remembered it was „Paris".

TOOTH / TEETH

have a sweet tooth *ein Leckermaul/eine Naschkatze sein* **B:** Mary is trying to lose weight, but she'll find it difficult keeping off the chocolates, she's got a sweet tooth.

lie through/in one's teeth *das Blaue vom Himmel herunterlügen* **A:** lie shamelessly **B:** George must have lied through his teeth when he told you he had won 3 million on the lottery last week, yesterday he asked me to lend him money for the taxi.

get one's teeth into something *sich in etwas hineinknien/festbeißen* **A:** put all one's energy/effort into it **B:** Our school physics book is very complicated, but if I want to pass the exam, then I'll just have to get my teeth into it.

be fed up to the (back) teeth *es mehr als satt haben* **A:** have one's stomach/belly full of it **B:** Since your mother came for a visit last week, she's only been complaining and criticising, I'm fed up to the teeth with the arrangement, next time she stays in a hotel.

clench one's teeth *die Zähne zusammenbeißen* **V:** grit one's teeth **A:** clench one's fist **B:** At fifteen years of age his parents were at a party and the house caught alight, but in spite of the smoke and flames, he clenched his teeth and got his baby brother safely out of the house.

be armed to the teeth *bis an die Zähne bewaffnet sein* **A:** be prepared to fight **B:** When the police saw the terrorists, holding hostages in the bank, were armed to the teeth, they dropped a tear gas bomb through the window, and saved serious injuries.

CLOTHING

BAG

it's in the bag *etwas so gut wie in der Tasche haben* **A:** It's virtually home and dry **B:** How was the interview for the job? – They're letting me know next week, but it's it in the bag, the director nodded to me when I left.

pack one's bags *seine Koffer packen* **A:** clear off **B:** If you don't like your stay with us, you can pack your bags any time you wish.

BELT

hit someone below the belt *jemandem einen Schlag unter die Gürtellinie versetzen* **V:** that's (a bit) under/below the belt **A:** make a mean/unfair attack or statement **B:** You needn't have hit him below the belt by laughing at him because he's deaf.

tighten the belt *den Gürtel enger schnallen* **V:** pull in one's belt **A:** tighten the strings **B:** You'll have to tighten the belt, son, my firm has put me on shorter hours so I'll have to reduce your student allowance.

BLOOMER

make a bloomer *einen dummen Fehler machen, einen Bock schießen* **A:** make a silly mistake **B:** I congratulated Susan on her recent marriage to George, and she walked out the office! – You made a bloomer there, George didn't turn up to the wedding.

BONNET

can stick it in your bonnet *sich etwas an den Hut stecken können* **A:** keep it **B:** You gave this Christmas present to your lover first but she didn't like it, well I don't want it either, you can stick it in your bonnet.

BOOT

give someone the boot *jemandem kündigen, jemanden her-

CLOTHING

ausschmeißen **A:** fire him **B:** No wonder the firm gave him the boot; in the six months he was there, when he wasn't ill, he always came an hour late.

lick someone's boots *jemandem die Stiefel lecken* **A:** get in with someone **B:** It won't help you licking the director's boots by opening his car door for him every morning, he's already chosen a successor for the managerial post.

CAP

a night-cap *ein Schlummertrunk* **Note:** can be used in a pub = the last drink or round, one for the road **B:** Before we go to bed, would you like a night-cap, a whiskey? – No, I've had enough alcohol, just a hot chocolate please.

That caps it all *Das ist die Krönung, das ist die Höhe* **V:** and to cap it all **A:** that puts the lid on it **B:** First he fouled the goal keeper, then he insulted the referee, and now he's been sent off, that caps it all!

COTTON

cotton on to something *etwas kapieren* **V:** (short) cotton on **A:** grasp something **B:** Well you cottoned on to the first chapter on physics very quickly, so we can start the second chapter.

CUFF

off the cuff *aus dem Handgelenk, aus dem Stegreif* **A:** at first glance **B:** Off the cuff, I'd say we should stop producing the product, but we should analyse the situation more carefully before finally deciding.

DRESSED

be dressed (up) to kill *aufgedonnert/aufgetakelt sein* **A:** be dressed/done up like a dog's dinner **B:** Since her husband left her she's been on the hunt for a man. – Yes I noticed that, she was in the super-market dressed up to kill.

GLOVE

fit someone like a glove *wie angegossen passen* **A:** fit someone to a „T" **B:** Since you've lost weight darling, your older clothes fit you like a glove.

HAT

keep something under one's hat *für sich behalten* **A:** keep it to oneself **B:** What I want to tell you, our boss told me in confidence, so keep it under your hat or the whole department will know about it.

do something at the drop of *etwas auf der Stelle/ohne Weiteres machen* **A:** do something without hesitation **B:** Jack is very helpful, when I asked him to drive me to the hospital, because my car was being repaired, he did it at the drop of a hat.

eat one's hat, if... *einen Besen fressen, wenn...* **A:** I'm a Chinaman **B:** If Jack wins the golf tournament today, after boozing all night on the party, I'll eat my hat.

pass the hat round (for someone) *den Hut herumgehen lassen* **V:** pass round the hat **B:** Her uncle sang so well at your wedding that we passed the hat round for him, but he put the money into her suitcase.

take one's hat off to someone *vor jemandem/etwas den Hut ziehen* **V:** raise one's hat to someone **A:** show someone your respect or admiration **B:** I must take my hat off to you, young man, for protecting that old lady from the three hooligans.

talk through one's hat *Quatsch/ dummes Zeug reden* **A:** talk throught one's head **B:** Don't talk through your hat, I lived in Spain for 3 years and they aren't all peasants or waiters, the Spanish people are proud and honourable, just as any nation.

PANTS

scare the pants off someone *jemanden zu Tode erschrecken* **A:** scare/terrify someone to death **B:** On our holiday, lighting candles when the electricity failed in the castle wasn't a problem, but Susan suddenly appearing with a sheet over her, scared the pants off me.

bore the pants off someone *jemanden zu Tode langweilen* **A:** bore someone **B:** For God's sake don't invite Admiral Haldane, he'll bore the pants off me with all his sea victories in the last war.

POCKET

pocket one's pride *seinen Stolz überwinden* **V:** swallow one's pride **A:** put one's pride in one's

CLOTHING

pocket **B:** The estate agent walked around my house criticising all the faults, but I pocketed my pride – we had to sell the house and he had a buyer already.

have something (already) in one's pocket *etwas schon in der Tasche haben* **A:** have it already in the bag **B:** Do you think Jack will get that top job? – Of course, with his connections, he's got the position already in his pocket.

RAG

feel like a wet rag *sich total ausgelaugt fühlen* **A:** feel all in **B:** I can't see you this evening, the water pipe burst and after the workers had left, I had to clean the whole flat, I feel like a wet rag.

go from rags to riches *vom Tellerwäscher zum Millionär* **Note:** usage often for women **B:** She was working in a cafe when a film producer saw her and sent her to Hollywood – she went from rags to riches in a year.

SHIRT

not have a shirt to one's back. *kein Hemd auf dem Leib tragen* **V:** not a shirt to his name **A:** unable to rub two pennies together **B:** I saw Jack the first time after 10 years, he didn't look at all happy. – No, he's just come out of prison and hasn't a shirt to his back.

keep one's shirt on *sich nicht aufregen* **A:** keep one's hair on **B:** You shouldn't have sent him shopping by himself, he's only nine! – Keep your shirt on, the shops are just round the corner and he's big enough.

SHOE

shake in one's shoes *vor Angst zittern* **A:** shake with fear, tremble with fear **B:** He shook in his shoes, when he heard the police knock at his house door.

be in someone's shoes *in jemandes Haut stecken* **V:** be in someone's skin **B:** I wouldn't like to be in his shoes, he was caught copying confidential information, and the boss wants a word with him.

put oneself in someone's shoes *sich in jemandes Lage versetzen* **V:** put oneself in his position **A:** see it his way **B:** He doesn't need to do a second job in the evenings. – Well, put yourself in his shoes, his wife has just lost her good job and is expecting her fourth child.

that's a different pair of shoes *Das sind zwei verschiedene Paar Schuhe* **A:** that's a another/different kettle of fish **B:** You and your brother both like your drink. – Well, I like an occasional beer, but with my brother that's a different pair of shoes, he gets drunk every day.

live on a shoe-string *von der Hand in den Mund leben* **A:** barely survive **B:** If he'd invested his winnings instead of spending like an idiot, he wouldn't be living on a shoe-string today.

SLEEVE

have something up one's sleeve *etwas in der Hinterhand haben* **V:** have a trick/some tricks up his sleeve **B:** I can't believe the salesman will give you so much for your car in exchange for buying a new one. – I'm suspicious too, he must have something up his sleeve.

SOCK

put a sock in it *Halt den Mund, hör auf!* **A:** hold your tongue **B:** Nagging at me for over an hour for losing my job won't change anything, put a sock in it!

pull one's socks up *sich am Riemen reißen* **A:** pull yourself together **B:** Your last school report was a disgrace, if you don't pull your socks up, you can forget university.

THREAD

hang by a thread *am seidenen Faden hängen* **V:** hang by a string **A:** hang in the balance **B:** After his terrible car accident, his life hung by a thread for nearly a week.

lose the thread of something *den Faden verlieren* **A:** lose the point, gist **B:** I'm sorry, but my thoughts were somewhere else and I've lost the thread of argument, could you repeat the basic points again.

pick up the threads (again) *den Faden wiederaufnehmen* **A:** pick up the pieces **B:** During his long illness, Alex couldn't work on his book; but I hope he can pick up the threads again.

TROUSERS

wear the trousers *die Hosen anhaben* **Note:** usually applied to women **A:** be the boss at home **B:** We haven't seen Mike and Mary for years, but last night at dinner it was obvious that she wears the trousers.

UPPERS

be (down) on one's uppers *auf den Hund gekommen sein* **A:** not have shirt to his back **B:** After he lost his home and wife he lost interest in everything, he's been down on his uppers for months, living like a tramp.

YARN

spin a (seaman's) yarn *ein Seemannsgarn erzählen/spinnen* **A:** tell a good/fantastic/great story **B:** You look bored son, why don't you go over to the neighbours, he's an old sea captain and can spin a yarn for hours.

COLOURS

BLACK

beat someone black and blue *grün und blau schlagen* **A:** beat someone up severely **B:** The drunken hooligans beat the old man (till he was) black and blue, and then ran off with his wallet.

BLUE

like a bolt from the blue *aus heiterem Himmel* **V:** out of the blue **A:** totally unexpected **B:** They had been happily married for 30 years, news of their divorce came like a bolt from the blue.

once in a blue moon *alle Jubeljahre einmal* **A:** do something very seldom **B:** I don't really care what my uncle thinks of me, he only visits me once in a blue moon.

wait (for something) until one is blue in the face *warten bis man schwarz wird* **A:** wait in vain, wait till the cows come home **B:** You obviously don't know our friend so well, if you've lent him money, then you can wait for it until your'e blue in the face.

cry blue murder *Zeter und Mordio schreien* **A:** make a huge rumpus **B:** If you take the baby's toy away, he'll cry blue murder.

COLOUR

be/feel/look off colour *unpässlich sein* **A:** look rather ill/poorly, **B:** You look (a bit) off colour, John, after the late night party and all that drinking, you ought to go to bed early tonight.

GREEN

be green with envy *gelb vor Neid sein* **A:** be very envious **B:** She was green with envy driving her Volkswagen, when her school friend overtook her in a Rolls Royce.

PINK

be tickled pink *sich wie ein Schneekönig freuen* **V:** be tickled to death **A:** relish/enjoy the situation **B:** She was tickled pink when her husband mistakenly put his underpants on back to front.

RED

catch red-handed *jemanden auf frischer Tat ertappen* **A:** catch him in the act **B:** As he opened the till, the police came into the shop and caught him red-handed.

WHITE

be as white as a sheet *kreidebleich, leichenblass sein* **A:** look very pale **B:** Have you seen a ghost, you're as white as a sheet!

white wash someone *1) jemanden reinwaschen, decken 2) jemanden spielend besiegen* **A:** 1) cover/stick up for him 2) easily beat someone **B:** 1) No good complaining to the Post about their telephone engineer, they'll only whitewash him 2) Against the school boxing champion you've no chance, he'll whitewash you.

YELLOW

be yellow *feige sein* **A:** be a coward, weakling, have no spunk **B:** Is George coming with us to meet the gang of hooligans who smashed our car windows? – No chance, he's yellow, he rang to say he was ill.

NATURAL ELEMENTS

AIR

vanish into thin air *sich ins Nichts auflösen, spurlos verschwinden* **A:** vanish into nothing **B:** George left the table during the meal in the hotel, and hadn't appeared when we were finished, we looked all over the hotel, but he'd vanished into thin air.

have a certain air about one *etwas an sich haben, ein gewisses Etwas haben* **A:** have/got that special something **B:** The new secretary is not particularly attractive, but she has a certain air about her, which makes you want to get to know her.

begrudge someone the (very) air he breathes *jemandem nicht die Luft zum Atmen gönnen* **A:** be envious of him **B:** When the man she always wanted to marry, visited her with his wife, she was extra polite to her, but inwardly begrudged her the air she breathed.

cut the air with a knife *Es herrscht dicke Luft* **A:** sense a state of tension **B:** Our guests started shouting very loudly, when we returned to the dining room they became suddenly quiet, but the tension was so high, you could have cut the air with a knife.

There's something in the air *Es liegt etwas in der Luft* **A:** There's something up/cooking **B:** There's something in the air, our finance director had 3 long meetings with the board members this week, and he was looking very ill today.

out of thin air *aus der Luft (greifen)* **A:** out of nothing at all **B:** Alexandra, I'm not a millionaire, how do you think I can find 10.000 pounds for a car for you, out of thin air?

be (still) in the air *in der Schwebe sein* **A:** be undecided **B:** Management still hasn't decided to dismiss 100 employees, because of protest from the trade union, so it's still in the air.

go up in the air *in die Luft/an die Decke gehen* **A:** lose one's temper **B:** My parents went up in the air, when I told them, after finishing school at 16, that I wanted to move into my boyfriend's flat.

clear the air *eine Sache/die Atmosphäre bereinigen* **A:** create a better atmosphere **B:** After the argument, Alex and Frank didn't talk to each other for days, then they finally discussed it and were able to clear the air.

CLOUD

Every cloud has a silver lining *selten ein Schaden ohne Nutzen* **A:** there's always a bright side to life/everything **B:** He was disappointed at losing his job, but with his redundancy pay he started his own business so every cloud has a silver lining.

EARTH

come down to earth *auf den Boden der Tatsachen kommen/ jemanden zurückholen* **V:** bring someone down/back to earth **A:** come down/back to reality **B:** After he realised acting was not his profession he came down to earth and started studying engineering.

feel like nothing on Earth *sich hundeelend fühlen* **V:** look, taste, smell, sound like nothing on earth **A:** (person) look/feel like death warmed up **B:** After his severe car accident, I visited him in hospital, he felt like nothing on earth.

pay the earth for something *ein Vermögen bezahlen* **A:** pay through the nose **B:** You must have paid the earth for that new Ferrari sports car.

What on earth *Was in aller Welt ...* **V:** Who, When, How, Why etc. on earth ... ? **A:** Who etc. in (the) Hell, in the World **B:** What on earth have you done to your hair, it's got more colours than the rainbow?

ELEMENT

brave the elements *den Elementen trotzen* **A:** defy the bad weather **B:** John was such a keen golfer, so in spite of the storm and torrential rain, he braved the elements and finished his round of golf.

FIRE

spread like wild fire *sich wie ein Lauffeuer verbreiten* **A:** circulate rapidly **B:** The minister's affair with the prostitute spread like wild fire.

NATURAL ELEMENTS

play with fire *mit dem Feuer spielen* **A:** ask for trouble, take a risk **B:** If Jack and his wife start arguing this evening, don't interfere or you'll be playing with fire; we'll just go into the kitchen and clear up.

ICE

put something on ice *auf Eis legen* **A:** put it aside **B:** We'll have to put your suggestion on ice for a while, the circumstances are not suitable at the moment.

skate on thin ice *sich auf dünnem Eis bewegen* **V:** walk on thin ice **A:** be on shaky ground **B:** Her boy friend has just left her after 4 years, so I wouldn't invite her to the disco this evening, you'll be skating on thin ice.

break the ice *das Eis brechen* **A:** loosen things up **B:** Due to tension in the near east, the government want to break the ice by improving relationships with Israel.

NATURE

become/be second nature to someone *jemandem zur zweiten Natur geworden sein* **A:** be/become a habit with him **B:** William has lied all his life, whether serious or in humour, he just can't tell the truth, it's become second nature to him.

OCEAN

be only a drop in the ocean *(nur) ein Tropfen auf den heißen Stein* **V:** a mere drop in the ocean **A:** not be worth talking about it **B:** John donated a pound for the restoration, but since the church required 200,000, it was only a drop in the ocean.

RAIN

Come rain or (come) shine *ob es regnet oder schneit* **A:** whatever happens **B:** Come rain or come shine, Alex visits her mother in hospital every evening after work.

raining cats and dogs *Es gießt in Strömen/wie aus Eimern/Kübeln/Kannen* **A:** It's pouring down **B:** You can forget our walk in the park, it's raining cats and dogs.

it never rains, but pours *(Ein) Unglück kommt selten allein* **B:** Our holiday hotel was cold and dirty, and on the third day our daughter was rushed to hospital with food poisoning, it never rains, but pours.

STORM

the calm before the storm *die Ruhe vor dem Sturm* **V:** lull before the storm (a lull in a conversation = a pause) **B:** The sky is still clear and the birds are singing, but I'll take the washing in, I think it's the calm before the storm, the weather is about to change.

a storm in a tea cup *ein Sturm im Wasserglas* **A:** make a mountain out of a mole-hill **B:** The whole commotion was just a storm in a tea cup, if you'd understood her correctly, she wasn't insulting you, but making a compliment.

SUN

make hay while the sun shines *Man muss das Eisen schmieden, solange es heiß ist* **A:** not miss your chance **B:** That's not typical of your husband, offering to buy you a new car; I'd make hay while the sun shines, if you wait too long, he'll change his mind.

WATER

still waters run deep *Stille Wasser sind tief* **V:** smooth waters run deep **A:** barking dogs seldom bite **B:** After our manager had that hefty argument with the Director, it's been very calm in the office, they apparently reached an agreement. – I'm not too sure, still waters run deep.

WIND

put the wind up someone *jemanden ins Bockshorn jagen* **A:** give him the creeps **Vulg:** give him the shits **B:** Don't put the wind up me by always saying the exam is very difficult. I've studied enough and have a fair chance of passing.

get the wind up *Angst bekommen* **A:** become alarmed or anxious **B:** We got the wind up, when Peter's bride still hadn't arrived at the church after 20 minutes, then Peter got an SMS saying she was caught in a traffic jam.

something is in the wind *etwas liegt in der Luft* **A:** sense something is up **B:** There's something in the wind Peter, the colleagues in the office have been whispering among themselves for the last week.

FOOD – DRINK

get wind of something *von etwas Wind bekommen* **A:** get a hint, feeling **B:** We got wind of his resignation a week before it appeared in the press.

take the wind out of someone's sails *jemandem den Wind aus den Segeln nehmen* **A:** forestall someone **B:** The government will admit their mistake and thus take the wind out the sails of the opposition.

FOOD – DRINK

APPLE

be the apple of somone's eye *etwas wie seinen Augapfel hüten* **A:** be the number one in someone's eyes **B:** Between father and daughter, the daughter can generally do no wrong. He loves his sons, but she is the apple of his eye.

upset the apple cart *alles über den Haufen werfen* **V:** upset the horse's cart **A:** spoil a situation/plan **B:** Your colleagues are still on strike for the next three days, so don't go into work tomorrow, or you'll upset the apple cart.

BACON

save someone's bacon *jemandem das Leben/die nackte Haut retten* **A:** save someone's neck/life **B:** A good job you pulled me back in time to avoid that fast oncoming car; you certainly saved my bacon, can I buy you a meal?

BEAN

be full of beans *sprühen vor Freude* **A:** bounce with joy **B:** She was full of beans yesterday, did she win the lottery? – No, but her doctor confirmed she was at last pregnant after waiting so long.

spill the beans (about) *etwas ausplaudern* **A:** let the cat out of the bag **B:** My decision to get married was a secret, only you and our sister knew. – I know, but she spilt the beans at school yesterday, it will be all over town by now.

BEEF

beef about *meckern, nörgeln* **A:** nag, moan **B:** Stop beefing all the time about my dress, if you earned more money then I could buy a new one.

BITE

bite off more than one can chew *sich zuviel zumuten* **A:** take on more than one bargained for **B:** If you'd let us help you, instead of trying to prepare the party alone, then everything would have been ready by now; you bit off more than you could chew.

BREAD

earn his daily bread *sein Brot/ seine Brötchen verdienen* **A:** earn your living **B:** Harry has no taste in clothes at all. – Well, at least he earns his daily bread, you don't even make an effort to find a job.

BUTTER

look as if butter wouldn't melt in his mouth *aussehen, als ob man kein Wässerchen trüben könnte* **A:** looks/seems too good to be true **B:** In court, the accused looked as if butter wouldn't melt in his mouth, but the jury knew he was the murderer.

butter someone (up) *Honig um den Bart schmieren* **A:** win someone over **B:** He buttered his boss by translating his speech in the evening, hoping for a salary increase.

CAKE

can't have your cake and eat it *Man kann nicht zwei Dinge auf einmal haben* **A:** can't have both ends of the stick **B:** I'd like to buy a car with the prize money, but we also need to decorate the house. – Well, make a decision, you can't have your cake and eat it.

piece of cake *ein Klacks, ein Kinderspiel* **A:** dead easy/simple **B:** The exam was a piece of cake, perhaps I was lucky and just the right questions came up.

a slice of the cake *ein Stück vom Kuchen (wollen)* **A:** a share of **B:** The market for mobile telephones is growing so fast, we ought to enter the market and get a slice of the cake as well.

go like hot cakes *weggehen wie warme Semmeln* **A:** be snapped up in no time **B:** That was the last CD of the newest album from Robbie Williams in the shop, they went like hot cakes.

CORE

be rotten to the core *durch und durch schlecht sein* **A:** be bad through and through **B:** He's fooled you with his politeness all

FOOD – DRINK

the time, you shouldn't marry him, he's rotten to the core.

CUCUMBER

be/remain/keep as cool as a cucumber *seelenruhig sein, die Ruhe selbst sein* **A:** keep calm cool and collected **B:** When thunder and lightning began most of the children got excited, but Susan was as cool as a cucumber, and continued reading.

EGG

egg someone on *jemanden anstacheln* **A:** push/put someone into trouble **B:** Don't egg him on like that, you know he'll be in trouble when a teacher catches him putting glue on all the door handles.

put all one's eggs in one basket *alles auf eine Karte setzen* **A:** stake everything on it **B:** When he got the huge lottery win, he made the mistake of putting all his eggs in one basket by buying only shares; he should have invested in different things.

FAT

live off/on the fat of the land *in Saus und Braus leben* **A:** live like a king **B:** They inherited a fortune and lived off the fat of the land for years, and eventually died through excessive eating and drinking.

the fat is in the fire (now) *der Teufel ist los* **A:** (all) hell will break loose **B:** The fat is in the fire now, son, your father has got this month's telephone bill; can't you find a girl in the town instead of one living in America?

FIG

not care/give a fig for *sich nichts aus etwas machen, einen Dreck darum kümmern* **A:** not care less/at all **B:** I don't care a fig for his opinion on the government, he's always lying and changing his mind.

GOOSEBERRY

play the gooseberry *das fünfte Rad am Wagen sein* **A:** not be wanted **B:** Even if I'm your older brother, I'm not going with you and your new boy friend to the cinema, I don't want to play the gooseberry.

JAM

money for jam *nachgeworfenes Geld* **A:** easy money **B:** That was money for jam, I just walked down the street and smiled, and the film director gave me a 100 Euros.

LOAF

half a loaf is better than none *besser als nichts* **V:** half a loaf is better than no bread **B:** After the war when food was scarce, we often had little to eat, but our mother reminded us, that half a loaf is better than none.

MEAL

don't make a meal of it *Übertreibs mal nicht* **V:** there's no need to make a meal out of it **A:** don't overdo it, don't go over the top **B:** I know, it was my fault, but don't make a meal of it, everyone can make a mistake, let's forget it now.

MEAT

one man's meat is another man's poison *Des einen Freud, des anderen Leid* **A:** what's good for one, is not good for the other **B:** His second wife is far more attractive than his first one. – I found his first wife was lovely, but one man's meat is another man's poison.

make mincemeat (out) of someone/thing *Hackfleisch aus jemanden machen* **A:** stone someone alive **B:** If he catches you with his wife, he'll make mincemeat out of you. He stopped shouting, when she made mincemeat of his arguments.

MILK

There's no use crying over spilt milk *Was passiert ist, ist passiert; hin ist hin* **V:** It's no good crying over spilt milk **A:** we can't undo the past, what's done is done **B:** Stop feeling sorrow for yourself at failing the first interview for a job, there's no use crying over spilt milk, concentrate on the next two interviews you have.

MUSTARD

be as keen as mustard *Feuer und Flamme sein* **A:** be wild about **B:** Do you think she'll pass her final pilot exam? – Of course, she's keen as mustard about flying.

NUT

be off one's nut/be nuts *etwas an der Birne haben, spinnen, verrückt sein* **A:** be off one's head, rocker, be bonkers **B:** How can you leave all your money on the bus, are you nuts?

FOOD – DRINK

be a hard/tough nut to crack *eine harte Nuss zu knacken sein* **B:** Jack's last offer for your car was 500 pounds, and you want double that amount, then good luck, he's a hard nut to crack.

go nuts *überschnappen, durchdrehen* **A:** go mad **B:** I'm not surprised he went nuts, when he saw the burglars had destroyed his expensive stereo and television set.

NUTSHELL

put it in a nutshell *um es kurz und bündig zu sagen* **V:** (short) in a nutshell **A:** put/say it short and sweet **B:** To put it in a nutshell, if we can't double our profits by the end of the year, we're all out of a job.

OIL

pour oil on troubled waters *die Wogen glätten* **A:** resolve differences **B:** With a joke just at the right time, the host was able to pour oil on troubled waters, and prevent a hefty argument among his guests.

burn the midnight oil *bis spät in die Nacht arbeiten, Nachtschicht einlegen* **A:** work late into the night **B:** He hasn't prepared his presentation for tomorrow yet, he'll be burning the midnight oil tonight.

PEANUTS

That's peanuts *Das sind kleine Fische* **A:** That's nothing **B:** I lost my wallet this week, containing 80 pounds. That's peanuts, I lost 80.000 this morning on the stock exchange.

PEAS

be as like as two peas in a pod *sich gleichen wie ein Ei dem anderen* **V:** be like two peas in pod **A:** look/be the split image of each other **B:** The research in gene technology and cloning has got so far that the copy and the original animal are as like as two peas in a pod.

PICNIC

it was no picnic *kein Honigschlecken sein* **A:** wasn't exactly a holiday **B:** I can imagine you experienced a lot of hardship during the war. – Well, I can tell you one thing, it was no picnic.

PIE

as easy as pie *kinderleicht* **A:** dead easy **B:** You were quick with the crossword puzzle. – Yes, it was easy as pie, but it will doubtless be a difficult one in tomorrow's newspaper.

POTATO

drop someone/something like a hot potato et*was/jemanden fallenlassen wie eine heiße Kartoffel* **A:** write someone off (as a bad job) **B:** He was lined up for promotion, but when the company discovered he was an alcoholic, they dropped him like a hot potato.

SALT

rub salt in the wound *Salz in die Wunde streuen* **A:** make it/things worse **B:** You've reduced her allowance, because she's not taking school seriously, but you'd be rubbing salt in the wound, if you told her she's not coming on holiday with us.

be worth his salt *sein Geld wert sein* **A:** worth his weight in gold **B:** The salary our director gets is ridiculously high, but he's worth his salt; I wouldn't like his responsibility and working all hours of the week and weekends.

take it with a pinch/grain of salt *nicht ganz wörtlich nehmen* **A:** believe it only in part **B:** I would take his story about recently buying a villa in Spain with a pinch of salt, he's been out of work for two years.

SARDINES

be like sardines in a tin *wie die Ölsardinen* **A:** be cramped for space **B:** This evening was particularly full in the underground train, we were like sardines in a tin, I couldn't even get my handkerchief out to blow my nose.

SOUP

be in the soup *in der Tinte sitzen, in der Klemme stecken* **A:** be in trouble **B:** We're reaching the border and customs are very strict here, so we'll be in the soup, if we can't find our passports.

STEW

stew in one's own juice *ihn (im eigenen Saft) schmoren lassen* **V:** let him stew in his own juice **A:** have to answer to one's own actions **B:** I've always helped you, but stealing is going too far; when the police come, I'm not helping you, you can stew in your own juice.

SPORTS – GAMES

be in a stew *in der Tinte sitzen, in der Klemme stecken* **A:** be in a mess/muddle **B:** He's in a stew at the moment, his wife is coming today and he hasn't cleaned the house nor washed the kids for 2 weeks.

TEA

not be (quite, exactly) one's cup of tea *nicht jemandes Sache sein* **A:** not be my sort of thing **B:** I turned down the well-paid job at the bank, because working at a computer 8 hours a day wasn't my cup of tea.

that's another cup of tea *etwas ganz anderes sein* **A:** be (totally) another matter **B:** We're talking about which private school would be the best for our daughter, what they cost and whether we can afford it, is another cup of tea.

would not do it for all the tea in China *etwas für alles Geld der Welt nicht tun* **A:** would not do it at all **B:** Our neighbours are very sweet, but are so messy and dirty, I wouldn't spend a holiday with them in the same apartment for all the tea in China.

SPORTS – GAMES

BACK-PEDAL

to back-pedal *einen Rückzieher machen* **A:** be (suddenly) against it **B:** Our neighbours promised to take our dog while we're on holiday, now they've back-pedalled, so we can cancel our holiday.

BALL

keep the ball rolling *etwas in Gang halten* **A:** keep things running **B:** At the shareholder's meeting, the Chairman, after a lengthy speech, kept the ball rolling by allowing each person to voice their opinion.

the ball is in your court *Jetzt bist du an der Reihe* **A:** the next step is yours **B:** I've given you my suggestion on the price our customer should pay, so as purchasing director the ball is now in your court.

BAT

do something off someone's own bat *etwas tun auf eigene Faust* **A:** do something on/of his own accord **B:** Instead of taking his parent's car to the garage as requested, he repaired it off his own bat.

BAY

keep someone/thing at bay *in Schach halten, (provisorisch) hinhalten* **A:** soothe/calm him/it for the moment **B:** The tablets will keep the pain in your broken arm at bay until you get to the hospital.

BOAT

sit/be in the same boat *im gleichen Boot sitzen* **B:** There's no point complaining about the bad weather during the golf tournament, the other players were sitting in the same boat.

rock the boat *etwas ins Wanken bringen, für Unruhe sorgen* **A:** make everyone unsure **B:** Our department was working well together, until the new assistant started rocking the boat by criticising most of the staff.

miss the boat *den Zug/den Anschluss verpassen* **A:** miss the bus **B:** I should have left our company years ago and joined a small consultancy firm, but at 55 I'm too old, I've missed the boat.

Catch

CARDS

be given one's cards *ihm wurde gekündigt* **A:** lose one's job **B:** After hitting the manager, he was given his cards.

have/hold all the cards in his hand *alle Karten/Trümpfe in der Hand haben/behalten* **A:** have the stronger hand **B:** Forget going to him about a salary increase, he's holding all the cards in his hand; he's the boss, the business is going badly and he's not satisfied with your performance.

put/lay one's cards on the table *seine Karten offen auf dem Tisch legen, mit offenen Karten spielen* **A:** show one's cards **B:** I still don't know why we both had to leave the company, why don't we lay our cards on the table, and find the real reason.

CATCH

catch someone out *jemanden bei etwas/auf frischer Tat ertappen* **A:** find someone in the act of (doing wrong) **B:** Jack went to the cinema instead of going to school, but his teacher had a day off and by chance was in the same cinema and caught Jack out.

SPORTS – GAMES

CHECK

hold in check *in Schach halten* **A:** keep/hold under control **B:** The slow economic growth should be able to hold price inflation in check. The terrorist kept the aeroplane passengers in check with a hand grenade.

GAME

be game for anything *zu allen Schandtaten bereit sein* **A:** will/would do anything **B:** Of course my wife would like to come with us on the mountain climbing holiday, she's game for anything.

be out of the game (for good) *weg vom Fenster sein* **A:** be finished **B:** The minister was hoping to win the local elections, but when the press discovered his illegal business transactions, he was out of the game (for good).

be off one's game *nicht in (seiner besten/üblichen) Form sein* **A:** not be in/on (his usual/best) form **B:** He's been off his game for nearly a month, let's hope he finds his form before the cup final next Saturday.

have an easy game to play *ein leichtes Spiel haben* **A:** have the game in one's hands **B:** The defending lawyer had an easy game to play in court, the witnesses were unconvinved from the start that his client was guilty.

the game is up *Das Spiel ist aus* **A:** that's the end of that **B:** The bank robbers were packing the money into suitcases, when they heard the police arrive. The gang leader said, sorry lads, the game's up.

play the game *nach den Regeln/ehrlich spielen* **A:** play fair **B:** Play the game, Jack, if you don't take those cards out of your sleeve, then I'm not playing poker with you again.

two can play at that game *Man kann den Spieß auch umdrehen* **A:** What you can do, I can do **B:** If you tell mummy I didn't go to school today, then two can play at that game, I'll tell her you went to that party last night and came home at 4 in the morning.

spoil someone's little game *jemandem die Suppe versalzen, sein Spiel verderben* **A:** put an end to his messing/joking around **B:** He's in the changing room again while our team is playing, hiding all the towels as he did last week; well, we'll soon spoil his little game, he gets a cold shower and goes home wet.

beat someone at his own game *jemanden mit seinen eigenen Waffen schlagen* **A:** outsmart someone doing the same thing **B:** Tom always cheats at maths by having a small piece of paper with him with the formulas. – Well, why don't you beat him at his own game, and write the formulas on your finger nails.

play games with someone *sein Spiel mit jemandem treiben, ins Lächerliche ziehen* **A:** make fun of someone **B:** I don't believe you that we were just photographed on the motorway, you're just playing games with me to make me drive more slowly.

JUMP

be one jump ahead *einen Schritt voraus sein* **V:** be one step ahead **B:** The consumer test for our new product was positive, we can start production. – Think again, our competitors were one jump ahead, their product is already in the supermarkets.

jump the gun *sich übereilen, voreilig sein* **A:** be a little too quick **B:** The building contractor jumped the gun by ordering the windows before the walls had been finished.

LEAP

be a leap in the dark *ein Sprung ins kalte Wasser* **A:** be a shot in the dark **B:** Whether the economy is bad or good, starting up your own business is always a leap in the dark.

do by leaps and bounds *sprunghaft* **A:** do it quickly, rapidly **B:** Since taking private lessons, his knowledge of English has improved by leaps and bounds.

LURCH

leave someone in the lurch *jemanden im Stich lassen* **A:** leave someone helpless **B:** He only wanted to borrow two pounds for a present for his mother's birthday, why did you refuse and leave an old friend in the lurch?

MARK

make one's mark *sich einen Namen machen, sein Ziel erreichen* **A:** make a name for oneself **B:** He certainly made his mark in the

SPORTS – GAMES

company, he was a board member at the age of thirty five.

hit the mark *ins Schwarze treffen* **A:** get something dead right **B:** The fortune teller hit the mark, when she told Alice she'd go to Italy within a week – two days later she won a prize for a holiday in Rome.

leave one's mark on/upon something *einer Sache seinen Stempel aufdrücken, seine Spur hinterlassen* **A:** make a (lasting) impression on **B:** After the factory had been closed down, it still left its mark on the people and village for many years to come.

overshoot the mark *über die Stränge schlagen, zu weit gehen* **A:** go over the top/limit **B:** Well, you overshoot the mark with finances this year, didn't you? You spent 400 pounds more than your yearly student grant.

be near to the mark *nah/näher am Ziel sein* **A:** be almost (more) correct **B:** When the economists predicted unemployment would remain around 5 million for this year, they were nearer to the mark than they realized.

be wide of/off the mark *weit vom Ziel sein, am Ziel vorbei* **A:** be well out **B:** You won't get a thousand pounds for your necklace, the auctioneer's estimate was wide of the mark, it's not worth half that price.

PEG

take/bring someone down a peg *jemandem einen Dämpfer verpassen* **V:** take/bring him down a notch/inch (or two) **A:** pull him down to size **B:** That new young manager is talking to everyone as if he were head of department; I'll have to take him down a peg.

be off the peg *von der Stange (etwas kaufen)* **B:** That new summer dress of yours looks really smart, was it tailor-made or off the peg?

PLAY

play along with *sich mit jemandem/etwas arrangieren/ auf etwas (scheinbar) eingehen* **A:** play his tune **B:** I'm sure Jack is stealing money, but he denies it flatly. – Well, I'd play along with him and wait until you catch him doing it.

play someone off against another *einen gegen den anderen ausspielen* **V:** (to example) he's trying to play us off against each other **B:** Our son told me you'd allowed him to go to the disco. – He's trying to play me off against you, we'll have to inform each other of what he says.

play hard to get *sich unnahbar geben* **A:** make out one is disinterested **B:** I've invited her 4 times for an evening meal this month, and she had an excuse each time. – Keep trying, I think she's interested, but she's just playing hard to get.

play something down *etwas runterspielen, verharmlosen* **A:** make less of it **B:** When the press printed the story of the minister's love affair with an actress, he played it down, saying they were only friends.

play for love *um die Ehre spielen, zum Spaß spielen* **A:** play (just) for the enjoyment of it **B:** Jack wants to play Bridge with us, but he only plays for money; we'll have to make it clear to him that we only play for love.

play on/upon words *mit Worten spielen, ein Wortspiel machen* **A:** use words with a double meaning **B:** I thought my English was pretty good, but I didn't understand that joke – it was difficult because George was playing on words.

POLE

not touch someone with a barge pole *jemanden nicht einmal mit der Kneifzange anfassen* **A:** not touch someone with a pair of tongs **B:** She looks so dirty, I wouldn't touch her with a barge pole.

RING

run rings/circles round someone *jemandem weit überlegen sein* **A:** beat someone hands down **B:** I wouldn't challenge the new club member to a game, he'll run rings round you; he was a tennis trainer in the USA before returning to Germany.

ROPE

learn/know the ropes *sich einarbeiten/sich (in etwas) auskennen* **A:** learn/know the tricks of the trade **B:** Before you start using the dredger on the building site, you've got to learn the

SPORTS – GAMES

ropes, digging out earth is not as easy as you think.

show/teach someone the ropes *jemanden in etwas (genau) einweihen* **A:** show/teach him the tricks of the trade **B:** George, the new apprentice starts today, show him the ropes, and let me know the results at the end of week.

RUN

be on the run *auf der Flucht sein* **A:** be still at large **B:** The escaped prisoners are still on the run, but the police informed the press that their hiding place has been located.

run someone down *jemanden schlechtmachen/runtermachen* **A:** speak ill of someone **B:** There's no need to run the young man down, the accident wasn't his fault, he was driving slowly and the child suddenly rushed out between two parked cars.

be in the running for *im Rennen (für etwas) liegen/sein* **V:** (opposite) be out of the running **A:** they have him in mind for **B:** George will be happy when he hears the news; the boss has just told me he's in the running for the post as finance director.

RUT

be (stuck) in a rut *im (alltäglichen) Trott sein* **A:** stuck in a groove **B:** She needs a new job, she's been in a rut for years, same firm, same work and no chance of promotion.

SADDLE

saddle someone with *jemandem etwas aufbürden, ihm zur Last legen* **A:** burden someone with **B:** That was unfair of our neighbours when they went on holiday; doing their garden was one thing, but then they saddled us with their 2 nephews for a week.

sit/be (firmly) in the saddle *(fest) im Sattel sitzen* **A:** stick to his position **B:** You've got no chance of getting George out of the firm, even for insulting you; since his father became President, he's sitting firmly in the saddle.

SAIL

sail through something *etwas leicht/spielend schaffen* **A:** do something like a piece of cake, **B:** He prepared himself so well, that he sailed through his exams with no trouble at all.

be plain sailing *leichte Aufgabe, klare Sache* **A:** be (easy and) straightforward **B:** Do you see any problems when we double production? – No, we have the capacity and can do night shifts, it should be plain sailing.

SPORT

be a good/bad sport *fairer/ehrlicher Spieler, guter/schlechter Verlierer sein* **A:** be a fair/unfair sportsman/player **B:** His team lost the game against the league champions, but being a good sport, he congratulated the opponent's trainer for playing the better game.

SPUR

on the spur of the moment *ganz spontan* **A:** out of the blue **B:** I decided to visit them on the spur of the moment, but when I knocked at their door, the neighbours said they were on holiday.

STAKE

have a stake in something *einen Anteil an etwas haben* **A:** have a major interest/share in something **B:** Why is George so concerned about that company's performance? – Well, he's got a stake in the company; he's the major share holder.

put everything at stake *alles aufs Spiel setzen* **A:** risk everything **B:** When he got the tip to buy shares in the company, he put everything at stake, but unfortunately the company went bankrupt a month later.

be at stake *auf dem Spiel stehen* **A:** be at risk, endangered. **B:** Your new plan to invest 3 Million in a production plant in the Near East looks attractive, but if war breaks out, then the whole project is at stake.

STREAM

swim against/with the stream *mit/gegen den Strom schwimmen* **A:** swim with/against the tide **B:** I've decided not to strike! – Well, you'll be swimming against the stream, the Trade Union members have just agreed to strike.

STROKE

not do a stroke *keinen Strich machen* **A:** not to do a thing **B:** In his first year at University, it was only parties and sports, he didn't do a stroke of work.

SWEEP

make a clean sweep of *reinen Tisch machen, aufräumen* **A:** make a clean breast of **B:** He finally made a clean sweep of all his old papers and files, and was surprised how big his study was.

TROT

keep someone on the trot *jemanden auf Trab halten* **A:** keep someone busy/on the move/on the ball/on his legs **B:** You'll have to keep the new assistant on the trot, otherwise he'll get bored and start reading the newspaper.

be (always) on the trot *(dauernd) auf Trab sein, auf den Beinen sein* **A:** be (always) busy **B:** My summer job as tourist guide really exhausts me, I'm on the trot all day with the sightseers.

HOUSE – ARTICLES

BELL

that rings a bell *Das kommt mir bekannt vor, das erinnert mich an etwas* **A:** that sounds familiar **B:** John Wellington sent us a Christmas card, who is he? – That rings a bell, I'm not certain, but I think we met him on our last holiday.

be as sound as a bell *kerngesund sein* **A:** be fit as a fiddle **B:** In spite of his car accident, within 4 weeks he was as sound as a bell and on the tennis courts again.

BOTTLE

take to the bottle *anfangen zu trinken/saufen* **A:** hit the bottle **B:** It often happens that a man takes to the bottle, if he loses is wife.

BROOMS

new brooms sweep clean *Neue Besen kehren gut* **B:** make a first good impression **B:** Our new manager has ordered new computers for everyone, and organised a personal meeting with each staff member once a month – new brooms sweep clean.

BRUSH

brush someone off *jemanden abblitzen lassen* **V:** give someone the brush-off **A:** drop or reject someone **B:** I was waiting over an hour for her, then she brushed me off by ringing my mobilephone to say she didn't want to see me.

BUCKET

kick the bucket *ins Gras beißen* **A:** drop dead, hit the dust **B:** Fred was on 60 cigarettes and 2 bottles of whiskey a day, no wonder he kicked the bucket at thirty years of age.

CANDLE

burn the candle at both ends *mit seinen Kräften Raubbau treiben, sich übernehmen* **A:** overdo things completely **B:** I'm worried about his health, he's studying night and day for the exam; he's burning the candle at both ends, he should have started studying earlier.

CEILING

hit the ceiling with joy *vor Freude an die Decke springen* **A:** jump for joy **B:** When his publishers accepted his first novel, he hit the ceiling with joy.

CLOCK

not put the clock back *die Uhr nicht zurückdrehen können* **A:** can't go back in time **B:** If we hadn't concentrated on our own careers and more on our children, then they would have been more interested today in studying. – That might well be, but you can't put the clock back.

go/work like clockwork *etwas läuft wie geschmiert* **A:** run well/smoothly **B:** Our holiday with friends in Scotland went like clockwork, the organisation and planning was perfect.

FOUNDATIONS

the (very) foundations shake *Da wackelt die Wand* **A:** celebrate excessively **B:** If we win the cup final, then we'll have such a party here, the very foundations will shake.

FUEL

add fuel to the flames *Öl ins Feuer gießen* **A:** add fuel to the fire **B:** They are simply not suited for another, don't suggest they

HOUSE – ARTICLES

should visit a psychologist, you'll only be adding fuel to the flames.

GATE-POST

between you, me and the gate-post *unter vier Augen* **A:** just between ourselves **B:** Officially he lost his place in the team because he was out of form, but between you, me and the gatepost, he was thrown out after having an affair with the trainer's wife.

HOME

There's no place like home *daheim ist daheim, eigner Herd ist Goldes wert* **A:** there's nothing like (being) home **B:** We enjoyed our 2 week stay in Japan, but when we got off the plane in London, we both said: There's no place like home.

make yourself at home *sich wie zu Hause fühlen, es sich gemütlich machen* **A:** feel at home **B:** So glad you could make it, give me your coat and make yourself at home.

bring something home to someone *jemandem etwas klarmachen* **A:** press one's point home **B:** You'll have to bring it home to her, that biting her finger nails will ruin her chance at an interview for a job.

nothing to write home about *nichts Wichtiges/Besonderes* **A:** nothing special **B:** How was the film? Well, the acting was moderate, but the story was very weak – nothing to write home about.

HOUSE

bring the house down *stürmischen Beifall ernten* **A:** raise the roof **B:** On his first concert conducting the Royal Philharmonic Orchestra, he brought the house down, everyone stood up to applaud.

get on like a house on fire *zusammenpassen wie ein Paar alte Schuhe, ausgezeichnet miteinander auskommen* **A:** very suited to each other **B:** Thirty years together and never an argument? – That's Jack and Susie; they get on like a house on fire.

That's safe as houses *Das ist todsicher* **A:** be totally safe **B:** We should pitch the tent lower down the hill, a strong gale is expected tonight. – Don't worry, that's safe as houses, I've been camping for 20 years.

IRON

iron things out *etwas ausbügeln, ausgleichen, beseitigen* **A:** smooth out, calm down **B:** How stupid, I scratched a car leaving the car park at the supermarket! – Don't worry, our friend Jim is our insurance man, he'll soon iron things out.

strike while the iron is hot *das Eisen schmieden, solange es heiß ist* **A:** not miss your chance **B:** The sales are on for two days, but if you want the best bargains, I'd strike while the iron is hot and be there early on the first day.

KETTLE

a pretty kettle of fish *eine schöne Bescherung* **A:** a muddle or mess **B:** King Edward VIII was faced with the choice of giving up his loved one, Mrs Simpson, or abdicating. That was a pretty kettle of fish for him!

PAN

be a flash in the pan *ein Strohfeuer, einmaliger Erfolg* **A:** be a chance/single success **B:** The first film he made was a success, but it must have been a flash in the pan, because since then his films have been awful.

out of the frying pan into the fire *vom Regen in die Traufe kommen* **A:** go from bad to worse **B:** You left our company because you wanted more independence, how's your new job? – Out of the frying pan into the fire, I can't leave the office for two minutes without permission.

PATH

lead someone up the garden path *jemanden auf Glatteis führen/an der Nase herumführen* **A:** take someone for a ride **B:** He won't give you that job he promised, he's just leading you up the garden path, so he can borrow your car.

PICTURE

get a picture of *sich ein Bild davon machen* **A:** get an idea of **B:** So you can get a picture of the country you're visiting, I can lend you a very good book with excellent photos.

put someone in the picture *jemanden ins Bild setzen* **A:** inform him of the situation **B:** George is

HOUSE – ARTICLES

new to the project, can you put him in the picture on the work done so far and latest developments.

get the picture *im Bilde sein, Bescheid wissen* **A:** be in the picture **B:** Thanks for explaining the problem, I've got the picture and know what has to be done.

keep someone in the picture *jemanden auf dem Laufenden halten* **A:** keep him up to date **B:** I'm financing your project, so I'd like to keep me in the picture, in case problems arise during your research.

PIN

hear a pin drop *eine Stecknadel fallen hören* **A:** be dead quite/still **B:** The children were screaming and laughing until the headmaster suddenly entered the class room; it was so quiet, you could hear a pin drop.

PLATE

have a lot on one's plate *genug/viel am Hals haben* **V:** have enough/a lot on his hands/round one's neck **B:** Don't ask Jim to help you in the garden, he's got enough on his plate looking after his sister's three children this week.

POT

have pots of money *Geld wie Heu haben* **A:** be rolling in money/it **B:** She donated thousands towards the restoration of the church, she must have pots of money.

ROOF

hit the roof *an die Decke gehen* **V:** go through the roof **A:** explode with rage. **B:** I've been waiting 2 hours for my wife in front her hairdresser's, if she doesn't come soon, I'll hit the roof.

RUG

pull the rug from under one's feet *jemandem den Boden unter den Füßen wegziehen* **A:** cut the ground from under his feet **B:** He'd collected a long list of mistakes the new manager had made, and reported it to the director, who pulled the rug from under his feet, informing him the manager had resigned.

SHELF

be (left) on the shelf *eine alte Jungfer sein* **A:** be an old maid **B:** Jane has concentrated on her career for so long, I fear she's been left on the shelf.

SIEVE

a memory like a sieve *ein Gedächtnis wie ein Sieb* **A:** be forgetful **B:** Grandfather forgot my name again when I visited him, he's got a memory like a sieve.

SLATE

have a clean slate *eine reine/saubere Weste haben* **A:** has done nothing dishonestly **B:** Most of the local police were involved in the corruption scandal, but the director of forensic medicine seemed to have a clean slate.

SPONGE

sponge off/on someone *jemandem auf der Tasche liegen, schnorren* **A:** scrounge (money, cigarettes) off him **B:** I've just seen Joe through the cafe window; he's always sponging off me, we'll have to go to the other cafe down the road.

STONE

leave no stone unturned *nichts unversucht lassen* **A:** leave nothing to chance **B:** In his attempt to establish who murdered his daughter, the police inspector left no stone unturned.

be (only) a stone's throw from/away *nur einen Katzensprung/Steinwurf entfernt* **V:** within a stone's throw of **A:** within (easy) walking distance **B:** Is the station very far? – No, you can park your car here, it's only a stone's throw away, two minutes walk and you're there.

STRING

pull (some) strings for *Beziehungen spielen lassen* **V:** pull a few strings for **A:** use your contacts **B:** Jack, I must get this job at your company, you know the manager of the department can't pull some strings for me?

(with) no strings attached *ohne Haken* **A:** no drawbacks **B:** It seems a good job, company car and share of the profits, and no strings attached.

TABLE

the tables are turned *das Blatt hat sich gewendet* **A:** the tide has turned, the wind has changed (direction) **B:** They were just about to purchase their competitors, then the tables were

HOUSE – ARTICLES

turned when the monopolies commission stopped the takeover.

turn the tables (on someone) *den Spieß umdrehen, das Blatt wenden* **A:** swing it in the other direction **B:** At half-time Chelsea were losing 1–3, then they turned the tables on Bayern in the second half and won 4–3.

TILE

have a night out on the tiles *einen draufmachen, versumpfen* **A:** be on the booze all night **B:** During the exam in the morning David fell asleep; not surprising, he had a night out on the tiles.

TOOTH-COMB

go over with a fine tooth-comb *etwas genau unter die Lupe nehmen* **V:** examine it with a f. t-c. **A:** check it thoroughly **B:** When the financial director received queries from his tax adviser, he went over the books with a fine tooth comb.

TOWEL

throw in the towel *das Handtuch werfen, die Flinte ins Korn werfen* **V:** throw in the sponge **A:** give up **B:** In the third round of the fight, he was knocked down 4 times, so before the fifth round began, his trainer threw in the towel.

WALL

talk to a brick wall *gegen eine Wand reden* **A:** no point talking to him **B:** Once he's made his mind up, he keeps to it. If you try changing his decision, it will be like talking to a brick wall.

drive someone up the wall *die Wände hochgehen, auf die Palme bringen* **V:** that is enough to drive him up the wall **A:** make someone boil (with rage) **B:** I can tell you, if you ever get stones in your kidneys, then the pain will drive you up the wall.

the writing is on the wall (for) *die Stunde hat geschlagen* **V:** see/read the writing on the wall **A:** the danger is staring us in the face **B:** They're closing our department, the writing is on the wall; the firm is bankrupt and staff members are already looking for new jobs.

ILLNESS – HEALTH

ACCIDENT

by accident *zufällig* **A:** do something by chance/mistake **B:** Don't shout at Grandma for dropping the plate, she only did it by accident.

ACHING

be aching all over *Es tut mir alles weh* **A:** my whole body aches **B:** I need a nice sauna and massage after 4 hours skiing, I'm aching all over.

be aching to see someone *sich nach jemandem sehr sehnen* **A:** be longing/dying to see her **B:** We haven't seen each other since our romantic holiday in summer, I'm aching to see her again.

ALL IN

be all in *todmüde sein* **A:** be tired out **B:** I can't drive you to the super market this morning, I'm just back from my night-shift and I'm all in.

BAG

be like a bag of bones *nur Haut und Knochen sein* **A:** be like a skeleton **B:** After dieting for 6 months, he looked like a bag of bones.

BALD

be as bald as a coot *ein Glatzkopf sein* **A:** be totally bald **B:** I haven't seen David for 5 years, he's lost so much hair that's he's bald as a coot, I hardly recognised him.

BEAT

be dead beat *todmüde sein* **A:** be exhausted **Vulg:** be shagged (out) or nackered **B:** After reaching home after his non-stop 2 day car drive, he was dead beat.

BLIND

as blind as a bat blind *blind wie ein Maulwurf* **A:** be totally blind (sarcastically) **B:** Letting her drive you through the town is dangerous, she should have lost her licence years ago, she's as blind as bat.

be blind with rage *blind vor Wut sein* **A:** be blinded by rage **B:** Jack had just collected his new car and missed the red traffic lights; a lorry crashed into his car and ruined it, he was blind with rage.

ILLNESS – HEALTH

BREAD-LINE

be on the bread-line *von der Hand in den Mund leben* **V:** live on the bread-line **A:** live in poverty **B:** Until Jack found another job, his wife and 5 children were on the bread-line.

COLD

catch one's death of cold *sich den Tod holen* **A:** catch a very bad cold **B:** You'll catch your death of cold, if you go out in that flimsy outfit after just having a hot bath.

COUGH

to cough up *Geld herausrücken, blechen* **A:** pay up **B:** You promised to pay me back the money I lent you last month, I need it urgently so you'll have to cough (it) up by tomorrow.

CROPPER

come a cropper *auf die Nase fallen* **A:** come into great difficulties **B:** Speculating on the stock exchange can be dangerous, many have come a cropper and lost a lot of money.

DEAF

be as deaf as a door post *stocktaub sein* **V:** be a deaf as door nail **B:** Our neighbours above us must be as deaf as a door post, the sound from their television is louder than ours!

DOCTOR

be just what the doctor ordered *genau das Richtige* **A:** be exatly what's needed **B:** After 5 hours on the golf course in the hot sun, how about a cool beer? – Great, that's just what the doctor ordered!

DOOR

be at death's door *mit dem Tode ringen* **A:** be almost dying **B:** The operation on his lungs revealed that cancer had already spread to the brain, he's sadly already at death's door.

END

be at a dead end *am Ende sein* **A:** be at a lost **B:** We'll have to help Jack before he does something stupid, he's can't deal with all his problems, he's at a dead end.

FEEL

not feel onself *nicht auf der Höhe sein* **A:** not feel one's normal self **B:** I don't know whether it's the weather or something else, but could we postpone the tennis game, I don't feel myself today.

FIT

be/look fighting fit *kerngesund sein, in bester Verfassung* **A:** be (as) fit as a fiddle **B:** Jack reported sick today, and we've so much work in the office at present; that's funny, I saw him playing tennis this afternoon and he looked fighting fit to me.

ILL

be ill at ease *sich (sehr) unwohl fühlen* **A:** feel very uncomfortable, unsure **B:** When his boss invited him to dinner and he discovered that the woman he had been having a secret affair with was the boss's wife, he felt ill at ease all evening.

LIMB

be out on a limb *ganz allein dastehen, in einer gefährlichen Lage sein* **A:** be on his own (now) **B:** It was Jack's decision to jump into the sea to save the child, and since the coast guards are remaining on shore, he's out on a limb.

be a danger to life and limb *Gefahr für Leib und Leben sein, lebensgefährlich sein* **A:** be a threat to health and security **B:** I wouldn't go to that new doctor, our neighbour was prescribed the wrong medicine for the wrong illness, he's a danger to life and limb.

MARROW

be chilled to the marrow *durchgefroren sein* **A:** be chilled to the bone **B:** I can't watch the football game any longer, it's so cold, I'm chilled to the marrow, I'm going home.

MEDICINE

give someone a taste of his own medicine *jemandem etwas mit gleicher Münze heimzahlen, gleiches mit Gleichem vergelten* **V:** give him a dose/piece of his own medicine **A:** give him some of his own medicine back **B:** Well, if he let the back tyre down on your bicycle, give him a taste of his own medicine and let both the tyres down on his bicycle tomorrow.

PAINS

take pains to do something *sich (große) Mühe geben, etwas zu tun* **V:** be at all pains to, go to great pains to **A:** put everything in to it **B:** He took great pains to

ILLNESS – HEALTH

mend the picture frame, which you dropped; you shouldn't make such a fuss, because only the glass is scratched slightly.

PILL

swallow the bitter pill *in den sauren Apfel beißen* **A:** have to do it the hard way **B:** If your stomach pain doesn't improve, then you'll have to swallow the bitter bill, and have an endoscopic examination of your throat and stomach.

SICK

be sick to death of something *die Nase voll von etwas/jemandem haben* **A:** be totally fed up with something **B:** I'm sick to death of his lying. He said he'd recently been in the Bahamas and bought a new racing car, but he's been on social assistance for the last 2 years.

SNEEZED

That's not to be sneezed at *nicht zu verachten* **A:** not to be laughed at **B:** I don't know why you're complaining, your new job has a salary of £25,000 a year, and that's not to be sneezed at.

THIN

be as thin as rake *ein Strich in der Landschaft sein, dünn wie eine Bohnenstange* **A:** be very thin **B:** You really have to start eating more, young man, you look as thin as a rake.

WAY

be in a bad way *jemandem schlecht gehen, in schlechter Verfassung sein* **A:** be in a serious condition **B:** He's had a bad car accident, he should go to the hospital at once, he's in a bad way.

fall by the wayside *auf der Strecke bleiben, scheitern* **A:** be left at the roadside **B:** My father forced me to join an accountancy firm, but I was never good at figures, and after 3 months I fell by the wayside, and left the firm.

WEATHER

feel (a little, a bit) under the weather *angeschlagen sein* **A:** not be/feel his usual self feel depressed or slightly sick **B:** After the hefty argument with his wife last night, John felt a bit under the weather the following day.

WHACKED

be whacked (out) *todmüde/fertig sein* **A:** be dead tired/beat **B:** After finishing the Olympic marathon in the extreme heat, he was whacked out.

WRECK

be a nervous wreck *mit den Nerven am Ende sein, ein Nervenbündel sein* **A:** be a bundle of nerves **B:** You were right about Mary's three children, they haven't been brought up at all; I had them for the day, and now I'm a nervous wreck.

LIFE – DEATH – LUCK

AGE

live to a ripe old age *ein hohes Alter erreichen* **A:** live a long time **B:** She's never let things worry her and always lived healthy, she'll live to a ripe old age.

BLESSING

be a blessing in disguise *Glück im Unglück haben* **A:** be a gift from Heaven **B:** Jack didn't obtain a seat at University, but his father's friend offered him a super position in his company; that was a blessing in disguise for Jack.

count one's blessings *für das dankbar sein, was man hat* **A:** be happy/content with what one has **B:** Don't complain about not winning on the lottery; you should count your blessings, you've got a healthy and happy family.

CHANCE

see someone's chance (s) running away (from) *seine Felle davonschwimmen sehen* **A:** see his chance(s) fading away or diminishing **B:** In his final test flight to become a pilot, he saw his chance running away from him, as he approached the runway at double the permitted speed.

leave something (up) to chance *etwas dem Zufall überlassen* **A:** rely totally on chance or luck (Often as a warning: Don't leave everything to chance) **B:** He left everything (up) to chance, and was naturally disappointed when he failed the examination.

LIFE – DEATH – LUCK

DEAD

be dead against something *absolut gegen etwas sein* **A:** be vehemently or strongly opposed to something **B:** Since his wife drowned 2 years ago on holiday, Peter is dead against holidays by the sea.

in the dead of night *mitten in der Nacht* **A:** in the middle of the night **B:** Can I stay the night mum, it's 2 a.m. in the morning, and I don't feel like driving 40 miles in the dead of night.

be dead and buried *tot und begraben sein, darüber ist längst Gras gewachsen* **A:** be finished and done with **B:** I thought the quarrel you had with your brother over your father's testament was dead and buried, why have you started arguing again about it?

be as dead as a doornail *mausetot sein* **A:** be dead beyond any doubt **B:** Since the nearby atomic power station exploded two years go, this town has been as dead as a doornail.

DEATH

work oneself to death *zu Tode arbeiten* **A:** work until one drops **B:** After working himself to death, in order to meet the deadline for his project, he was certainly glad to go on holiday.

someone/it will be the death of me *Es bringt/Du bringst mich noch ins Grab* **V:** you/it will be the end of me **B:** Since my retirement, you find a fault with me every single day, if it goes on much longer, you'll be the death of me.

sign one's own death-warrant *sein eigenes Todesurteil unterzeichnen* **A:** destroy onself **B:** Your brother still thinks you were to blame for ruining the family firm, but he promised your father he would support you, so I wouldn't quarrel with him, or you've probably signed your own death-warrant.

DEVIL

talk of the devil *Wenn man vom Teufel spricht, kommt er auch* **A:** now look who's just appeared! We were just talking about you! **B:** Our new maths teacher is a miserable person, don't you think so John? – Talk of the devil, he's just coming into the classroom!

FAITH

act in good faith *im guten Glauben handeln, nach bestem Wissen* **A:** mean only well **B:** When the neighbours sold you their old washing machine, they acted in good faith, they didn't know it would break down after 4 months.

GHOST

give up the ghost *den Geist aufgeben* **A:** cease to function **B:** That old car of mine was faithful for nearly 10 years, and yesterday it gave up the ghost.

GOSPEL

take as/for Gospel *für bare Münze nehmen* **A:** take as the Gospel's truth **B:** I took it for Gospel when the doctor told me after the operation he would walk again; but after 3 years he's still in a wheelchair.

GRACE

give someone a day's grace *einen Tag Aufschub geben, jemanden ein bisschen mehr Zeit lassen* **V:** give someone a few days' grace **A:** give someone another day (still), a bit more time **B:** Your mother is shouting about her bad marriage and you are screaming about lack of money, give me a day's grace; we can talk about it tomorrow.

HEAVEN

be like heaven on earth *wie der Himmel auf Erden sein* **A:** be incomparable **B:** Compared with that old dirty hotel we booked for our last holiday, this new one is like heaven on earth.

stink to high heaven *zum Himmel stinken* **A:** be a public outrage, scandal **B:** The planning permission for a new chemical plant in the middle of the forest stinks to high heaven, there should be a public inquiry.

be in seventh heaven *auf Wolke Sieben schweben/im 7. Himmel sein* **A:** be up in the clouds **B:** Since Peter proposed to Anne, she' been in seventh heaven.

HELL

give someone hell *jemandem die Hölle heiß machen* **A:** give her a piece of one's mind **B:** When the parents found out that the babysitter had spent the evening in the disco instead of looking after their baby, they gave her hell.

LIFE – DEATH – LUCK

do (just) for the hell of it *aus Jux und Tollerei* **A:** do it just for fun **B:** When the police asked the youth why he'd exceeded the speed limit, he replied he' done it just for the hell of it.

To hell with something *zum Teufel mit etwas* **A:** I don't care a damm about **B:** To hell with your complaints; in order to pass my exams, I have to do piano practice at least 4 hours a day, show some neighbourly consideration.

Go to hell! *Geh zum Teufel! Du kannst mich mal!* **V:** To hell with you! **A:** clear off **B:** You told the boss I had problems with my marriage so you could get promotion, you're a fine friend – you can go to hell!

be hell-bent on something *versessen auf etwas sein* **A:** be absolutely determined on or obsessed with **B:** I'm worried about Jack, after his nasty car accident, he's still driving around like an obsessed idiot; he seems hell-bent on killing himself.

all hell is/will (be) let loose *der Teufel ist los* **V:** (Past form =) All hell broke loose **A:** be (in) a state of uproar **B:** When management doesn't give the workers the wage increase they promised them, then all hell will let loose.

LIFE

as large as life *in voller Lebensgröße* **A:** (person) in flesh and blood **B:** I was listening to a song from Mick Jagger in the music shop, and suddenly he walked in, (as) large as life.

someone can bet his life on it *Da können Sie Gift darauf nehmen* **A:** You can bet your last penny **B:** You can bet your life on it, that my ex-wife is not coming to my party, if she has any funny ideas about coming, then the party is cancelled.

lead a dog's life *leben wie ein Hund* **A:** lead a misaberable existence **B:** He's been leading a dog's life, since he lost his wife and his company.

run for (someone's) dear life *um sein Leben rennen* **A:** run out of sheer fright **B:** As the burglar saw Jack descending the stairs with a shotgun, he ran for dear life.

not for the life of me *nicht um alles in der Welt* **V:** Not on your life **A:** not to save my life **B:** I couldn't for the life of me imagine my brother entering a monastery, he values materialistic comfort too much. Could you mind our baby for a day? – Not on your life!

LIGHT

show in a different light *etwas in einem anderen Licht zeigen* **A:** show/reveal in a different light **B:** In the new book on Hitler's life, his way of thinking was shown by the author in a (totally) different light.

LIVE

live beyond/above one's means *über seine Verhältnisse leben* **A:** his style of living didn't fit his purse **B:** No wonder Family Smith went bankrupt, they have been living beyond their means for years.

live and let live *leben und leben lassen* **A:** be tolerant **B:** Stop worrying about who your 23 year old daughter is spending her free time with, live and let live.

You live and learn *man lernt nie aus* **A:** you never stop learning **B:** Who would have thought that the mayor's wife would be caught shop-lifting; you live and learn!

LUCK

not heard of his good luck (yet) *(ironisch) noch nichts von seinem Glück wissen* **A:** (ironical) hasn't heard his good news yet **B:** George's wife has invited her mother for a week's stay – poor George, he hasn't heard of his good luck yet.

have luck on one's side *das Glück auf seiner Seite haben* **A:** have a lucky period/spell **B:** John won a million on the lottery three months ago, and last week won two million, he certainly had luck on his side.

have the luck of the devil *unverschämtes Glück haben* **A:** have the devil's own luck **B:** He's got the luck of the devil, the stock exchange is at its lowest point, and although he invested in a dubious firm, the shares are climbing even higher.

count/consider oneself lucky *von Glück sagen können/sich glücklich schätzen* **A:** be thankful

LIFE – DEATH – LUCK

for having such luck **B:** You can count yourself lucky, that in your drunken state, the police didn't take you to the Police Station for a blood test.

MERCIES

be thankful for small mercies *sich mit Wenigem zufrieden geben* **A:** half a loaf is better than none **B:** Susan got a genuine Cartier watch for Christmas; well you can have mum's watch, she doesn't wear it anymore; it's not so exclusive, but be thankful for small mercies.

SAKE

For heaven's sake *In Gottes Namen, selbstverständlich* **A:** by all means **B:** For heaven's sake, take my car, if you don't think you'll get there on time by train.

For God's sake *Um Himmels willen!* **A:** in heaven's name **B:** For God's sake, take that box of matches out of the children's room, they could start a fire.

SAVE

(not) to save one's life *etwas beim besten Willen nicht tun* **A:** for the life of me **B:** Thanks, but I can't play tennis to save my life, have a game with my brother, he's very good.

MIND – FEELING

ABOVE

be above someone *es geht über meinen Verstand* **A:** be above/ beyond me **B:** What the Professor has been explaining for the last hour, is (totally) above me, I haven't understood a word.

ABSENCE

absence makes the heart grow fonder *mit der Entfernung wächst die Liebe* **A:** one's feelings get stronger the longer one is separated **B:** They had a huge argument, when he told her the Navy was transferring him to Asia for 6 months, but since then she's longing for his return – absence makes the heart grow fonder!

ACTIONS

Actions speak louder than words *Eine Tat zählt mehr als 1000 Wor-*

te **B:** You were always phoning her, why did she start going out with George? – Well, he took her a bunch of roses and went to the the theatre with her, actions speak louder than words.

BITTEN

once bitten twice shy *ein gebranntes Kind scheut das Feuer* **A:** not make the same mistake again **B:** Do you think George will invest in my new computer company? – Unlikely, he lost half a million last year buying shares in such firms; once bitten twice shy.

BORED

be bored stiff *sich zu Tode langweilen* **A:** be bored to tears **B:** My husband hates TV talk-shows, he gets bored stiff after a few minutes and goes to bed to read a book.

BOTTOM

get to the bottom of the matter *einer Sache auf den Grund gehen* **A:** get to the root of the matter **B:** Inspector, you've been working 3 weeks on the unsolved murders; I'm getting pressure from the minister, please get to the bottom of the matter by the end of the month.

BREATH

in the same (all in one) breath *im selben Atemzug* **A:** in the same moment **B:** She said she wanted to leave him and added in the same breath, that she still loved him.

waste one's breath *in den Wind reden* **A:** waste one's time **B:** You're wasting your breath offering him a job, the lazy rascal will continue to live on social security.

BROWNED

be browned off (with) *jemanden/etwas satt haben* **A:** be bored **B:** I'm browned off with this party, bad music and stupid people, I'm going home.

BYGONES

let bygones be bygones *Schwamm drüber/die Vergangenheit ruhen lassen* **A:** let us forgive and forget **B:** I'm sorry for having an affair with your sister, but after two weeks we both realised the relationship would lead to nothing. I love you just as much as before, can't we let bygones be bygones?

MIND – FEELING

CARE

I couldn't (don't) care less *Das ist mir völlig egal* **A:** don't/couldn't care a fig **B:** Your girlfriend, Jane, hasn't invited you to her party. – I couldn't care less, we had a huge argument last week and I've finished the relationship.

CLASS

be in a class of one's own *eine Klasse für sich sein, unvergleichbar sein* **V:** be in a class by himself **A:** be the very best **B:** If your husband is to have the best chance possible, there's only one brain surgeon who can help him, that's Professor Marlin, he's in a class of his own.

COMPLIMENTS

fish for compliments *auf Komplimente aus sein* **A:** look for praise or recognition **B:** I know you've already been offered the position of Director of our department, why are you asking me again, whether you're capable for the job, you're just fishing for compliments!

CONSCIENCE

have something on one's conscience *auf dem Gewissen haben* **V:** have something on one's mind **B:** Why did you hit your son for just eating your favourite chocolate? – Don't remind me, it's been on my conscience for days now.

be a matter of conscience *eine Gewissensfrage sein* **V:** be a question of conscience **B:** Why don't you send money to help the homeless children in Columbia? – Well, it's a matter of conscience, it's the government's responsibility to solve the problem, they get enough profits from their drug business.

CRYSTAL BALL

(be) crystal ball gazing *Wahrsagerei* **A:** look into the future **B:** I don't believe in all this crystal ball gazing, nobody can predict the future.

DAMPER

put the damper(s) on something *einen Dämpfer aufsetzen* **A:** pour cold water on something **B:** George was certain he would easily win the tennis tournament, but losing in the first round put the damper on his self-confidence.

DAWNED

something (it) dawned on someone *jemandem dämmerte etwas* **A:** it (suddenly) flashed across my mind **B:** Darling, there's no need to get dressed for the party, it's suddenly dawned on me, that Jack rang last night to say he's postponed the party until next Saturday.

DREAM

go like a dream *laufen wie geschmiert, traumhaft* **A:** go/run perfectly **B:** I was a little worried about buying George's car without driving it first, but I drove for an hour on the motorway today and it went like a dream.

would not dream of doing *wäre mir nicht im Traum eingefallen* **A:** never dreamed (dreamt) of such a thing **B:** Jack, I'll be back in an hour, keep your fingers out of the cash box. – I wouldn't dream of doing such a thing, boss, you were the only one who gave me a job after leaving prison.

DUMPS

be in the dumps *niedergeschlagen sein* **A:** be down **B:** When she lost her husband and her only son got married, she was really in the dumps, until she met a nice partner.

EARNEST

in dead earnest *in vollem Ernst* **A:** for dead certainy **B:** I can't believe Jack's going into a monastery. – He means it in dead earnest, after losing his wife last month, he sees no purpose in living in the normal world.

EXCUSE

be a lame excuse *eine faule Ausrede* **A:** be a weak excuse **B:** I'm sorry I was late in the office this morning, but I had trouble finding my socks. – Well, that's a lame excuse!

FANCY

take a fancy to someone/thing *Gefallen finden an* **V:** fancy someone/thing **A:** take a (sudden/instant) liking to **B:** The moment the new secretary walked into the office, Jack took a fancy to her and promptly invited her for an evening meal.

catch someone's fancy *jemandes Interesse wecken, ihm gefallen* **A:** tickle/take someone's fancy **B:** The attractive secretary certainly caught Jack's fancy,

MIND – FEELING

since she joined us he's been taking every opportunity to help her.

FEAR

there's no fear of ... *es ist nichts zu befürchten/es ist sehr unwahrscheinlich, dass...* **V:** there's not much fear of **A:** it's very unlikely that **B:** There's no fear of our losing our jobs, the company has just invested in an extension to the production plant.

FED UP

be fed up with something *Nase voll von etwas/jemandem haben* **A:** be sick to death of/with **B:** He was fed up with his holiday in Spain, after it had continually rained for three weeks.

FEELINGS

vent one's feelings on someone *seinen Gefühlen freien Lauf lassen* **V:** give vent to one's feelings **A:** make a clean breast with someone **B:** There's no need to vent your feelings on me because you didn't get a salary increase, shout at your boss!

no hard feelings *nichts für ungut* **A:** no ill-feelings, don't take it personally/to heart **B:** We've been close friends for over 20 years; no hard feelings, but you're just not qualified enough to apply for that job.

GET OFF

tell someone where to get off *jemandem gründlich seine Meinung sagen, jemandem sagen wo es lang geht* **A:** tell him straight to his face **B:** Jack offered to help with the painting, but never stopped correcting me, so I told him where to get off and reminded him it was my job for 20 years.

GIFT

be a gift from heaven *ein Geschenk des Himmels* **V:** gift from the gods **A:** be a godsend **B:** He'd been waiting for a heart implantation for 10 months, then the hospital informed him that a donor had been found, for him that was a gift from heaven.

have the gift of the gab *nicht auf den Mund gefallen sein* **A:** be a gifted/capable speaker **B:** Jack left his job at the bank and has become a salesman. – Well, he should be successful, he's certainly got the gift of the gab, he could sell books to a blind man.

HASTE

More haste less speed *Eile mit Weile* **A:** take it easy **B:** In the rush you didn't lock your suitcase properly, and it opened up before I got to the car; more haste less speed, darling, it took me 20 minutes to pack your suitcase again.

HOPES

pin one's hopes on *seine Hoffnung darauf setzen* **V:** pin one's faith on **A:** put/hang one's last hope on **B:** We're pinning our hopes on the latest American medicine to cure our son of his disease.

HUE

raise a hue and cry *Zeter und Mordio schreien* **A:** make/cause a public outcry **B:** When the government passed the law allowing abortions, many Catholics raised a hue and cry.

IDEA

run away with the idea *sich etwas in den Kopf setzen* **A:** jump to conclusions **B:** I've paid for your meal because you're short of money, but don't run away with the idea that I'll always be inviting you.

not have the faintest/foggiest idea *keinen Schimmer/Dunst von etwas haben* **A:** not have the faintest notion/idea **B:** Sorry, but I didn't have the faintest idea you were coming this evening for a meal, I'm off to tennis and my wife is with friends; check your calendar, we arranged to meet next Saturday.

play with the idea *mit dem Gedanken spielen, etwas zu tun* **V:** toy with **A:** let it go through my head **B:** I'm playing with the idea of selling the house and buying a bigger one, but I'll have to check with the bank.

LET DOWN

let someone down *jemanden im Stich lassen, hängen lassen* **A:** leave him in the lurch **B:** I promised to collect her from the airport, but let her down, I overslept and she had to take a taxi.

LIE

tell a white lie *eine Notlüge erzählen* **B:** Parents are sometimes in a situation, when they tell their children a white lie to save them from being very upset and disappointed.

MIND – FEELING

LOSS

be a dead loss *ein hoffnungsloser Fall sein* **A:** be useless **B:** Jack's language course was a dead loss, after 3 months he still couldn't speak a full sentence in Spanish.

LOVE

not for love nor money *nicht für Geld und gute Worte, um keinen Preis* **A:** not at/for any price **B:** When the international trade fairs are on, you can't get a hotel room in the city for love or money.

For the love of God *Um Gottes/ Himmels willen!* **A:** for God's sake **B:** For the love of God – don't start accelerating now, the traffic lights are already red!

MESSAGE

get the message *etwas kapieren, raffen* **A:** get the warning/ threat/point **B:** I'm telling you for the second time; he doesn't want anything more to do with us, he's left our club and found new friends, have you got the message now?

MIND

take one's mind off something *sich von etwas ablenken* **A:** leave one's worries behind (for a moment) **B:** Whenever my wife has worries, she always reads a good book to take her mind off her problems.

mind one's own business *sich um seine eigenen Angelegenheiten kümmern* **A:** don't pry into my private affairs **B:** I was talking with the postman this morning on salaries for top managers, then he asked me what I earned myself, I told him to mind his own business.

bear/keep something in mind *im Auge behalten, daran denken* **A:** pay heed to **B:** When you go to the shops with your brother, bear in mind he's only 6 years of age, so be careful crossing the road.

prey on one's mind *der Gedanke bedrückt/quält/beschäftigt ihn* **A:** weigh on one's mind **B:** After hitting the child while driving back home, it preyed on his mind for weeks, even though he wasn't to blame for the accident.

put someone's mind at rest *jemanden beruhigen* **A:** reassure someone **B:** During his wife's

Mind

operation, he was very worried, then the doctor put his mind at rest by saying everything was fine.

change/alter one's mind *sich anders besinnen/entscheiden* **A:** change one's opinion **B:** Why isn't John coming to the football match with us? – He changed his mind when it started raining, he's watching the game on TV.

cross one's mind *jemandem etwas einfallen, in den Sinn kommen* **A:** occur to one **B:** It just crossed my mind that you may have left your scarf in the toilet, why don't we go back to the restaurant, and you can check.

make up one's mind *sich entschließen/entscheiden* **A:** reach a decision **B:** You've been considering Italy or Spain for our summer holidays for over a month now, if you don't make up your mind soon, we won't get a booking at all.

set one's mind on something *fest entschlossen sein, sich anstrengen etwas zu tun* **A:** keep to one's decision **B:** That's ridiculous, wanting to study medicine at 55. – Well, you won't influence her, she's set her mind on it.

call to mind *sich daran erinnern* **A:** remember/recall **B:** I can't call to mind you telling me that you've invited the neighbours for this evening; I probably didn't register it with all the problems in the office.

slip one's mind *dem Gedächtnis entfallen* **A:** slip one's memory **B:** What are doing in your pyjamas still, my parents are arriving in an hour for lunch. – Sorry, it slipped my mind totally, that they were coming today.

read someone's mind *seine Gedanken lesen* **A:** know what someone is thinking (about/of) **B:** Why did our competitor start producing toilet paper instead of keeping to ashtrays. – Well, if I could read their minds, I'd be on the executive board of our company.

be/have something on one's mind etwas *auf dem Herzen haben* **A:** it has been worrying me **B:** That hefty argument with my brother has been on my mind for days, I ought to ring and

MIND – FEELING

suggest we meet for a drink to chat about it.

broaden one's mind *seinen Horizont erweitern, aufgeschlossener werden* **A:** broaden one's horizon(s) **B:** You won't learn very much staying here in the village; go abroad, learn a new culture and language, and broaden your mind.

not get it out of one's mind *etwas nicht aus dem Kopf bekommen* **A:** not get it out of one's head **B:** I still can't get it out of my mind that our lazy son got one of the best exam results in his class, after spending most of his time on the sport's field or at parties.

speak one's mind *seine Meinung äußern, frei herausreden* **A:** speak openly **B:** When you're at your interview, Alexandra, you shouldn't always think about what they want to hear; if you speak your mind, then your chances of getting the job are higher.

give someone a (good) piece of one's mind *jemandem ordentlich die Meinung sagen* **A:** give someone something to think about **B:** When he heard that the new boy-friend hadn't driven his daughter back home after the late night party, he gave the young man a piece of his mind.

have something in mind *eine bestimmte Vorstellung haben* **A:** have a specific idea **B:** We can offer town houses, cottages, villas, bungalows and flats, which type of house did you have in mind?

be a weight off one's mind *jemandem ein Stein vom Herzen fallen, sein Gewissen beruhigen* **A:** relieve one's mind **B:** When his mother had a severe illness, it was a weight off his mind, knowing his wife could take time off from work to look after her.

be out of one's mind *verrückt sein, nicht bei vollen Verstand sein* **A:** be out of her senses **B:** He must be out of his mind buying that new car, he doesn't earn enough to buy himself a bicycle.

be in one's right mind *bei vollen Verstand sein* **V:** No one in her right mind would/can **A:** be sane, be all there **B:** Are you sure she's in her right mind inviting 120 guests to her party, her flat is not big enough to take more than 6 or 7 people.

drive someone out of one's mind (with) *jemanden wahnsinnig/ verrückt machen* **A:** drive someone out of one's wits with **B:** When news came, that the birth had complications, and his wife and child were in a critical position, it drove him out of his mind with worry.

MISERY

put someone out of one's misery *jemanden aus seiner Qual erlösen* **A:** put an end to one's suffering/worries **B:** When the laboratory results arrived for his patient, he put her out of her misery, by phoning to tell her she hadn't got breast cancer.

OUTCRY

raise a general outcry *eine Welle des Protests verursachen* **A:** cause a wave of discontent **B:** A few years back, speaking openly about homosexuals raised a general outcry, today one regards the topic less emotionally.

PEACE

have no peace (of mind) *keine Ruhe/keinen Seelenfrieden haben* **A:** not be relaxed **B:** The roads are icy so drive carefully, and we'll have no peace of mind, until you've phoned us to say your back home safely.

POINT

be a sore point with *ein wunder Punkt sein* **V:** hit on a sore point **A:** be a sore/delicate spot with someone **B:** I wouldn't mention his father's company going bankrupt, it's a sore point with him.

have a dead point *einen toten Punkt haben* **A:** have a drowsy moment **B:** Jack invited us to his party, and he suddenly fell asleep for an hour and woke up fighting fit at midnight – Yes, he always has a dead point between 11 and 12 in the evening.

PRIDE

pride goes before fall *Hochmut kommt vor dem Fall* **B:** You shouldn't criticise people less fortunate than yourself, you could end up the same – pride goes before fall.

swallow one's pride *seinen Stolz überwinden, klein beigeben* **A:** pocket one's pride **B:** Although

MIND – FEELING

his mother wrongly blamed him instead of his brother for the accident, he swallowed his pride and apologised.

take (a) pride in *stolz auf etwas sein* **A:** do it with body and soul **B:** Is he suitable for visiting the elderly and sick? – Well, after 8 years caring for his dying mother, I think he takes a pride in helping the needy.

PURPOSES

talk at cross-purposes *aneinander vorbei reden* **A:** not talking about the same thing **B:** We've been talking at cross-purposes for the last 10 minutes, I said you will inherit half of our parent's wealth, and you understood half of mother's wealth.

QUALMS

have no qualms about *keine Skrupel/Bedenken haben* **A:** have no hesitation or bad/guilty conscience **B:** If a wild dog were not on it's lead and attacked me, I wouldn't have any qualms about defending myself.

RAGE

be all the rage *der letzte Schrei sein* **A:** be the fashion/trend **B:** As youngsters we had roller skates, but those lads rushed past us wearing shoes with wheels! – Oh, you mean in-line skates, they're all the rage now.

fly into a rage *in Wut geraten, einen Wutanfall bekommen* **A:** explode wit anger **B:** When the neighbour's dog ruined the bed of roses in his front garden, he flew into a rage.

RAY

a ray of hope *ein Hoffnungsschimmer* **A:** glimmer of hope **B:** In spite of the complicated operation after the car accident, the doctor gave the patient a ray of hope, by saying he had a 50 to 60% chance of walking again.

REASON

there is every reason to believe *alles spricht dafür, guten Grund haben zur Annahme, ...* **A:** there is good/ample reason to believe **B:** The missing minister has still not been found, but in view of his parents living in Madrid, there is every reason to believe he is somewhere in Spain.

bring someone to reason *jemanden zur Vernunft bringen* **A:** get someone to think rationally **B:** The policeman approached the confused man standing on the window edge of the 12th floor, and tried to bring him to reason.

listen to reason *auf die Stimme der Vernunft hören* **A:** follow someone's words/advice **B:** Going to the party in that thin summer dress in the middle of winter was silly; your mother warned you and if you'd listened to reason, you wouldn't be ill in bed now.

REGRET

live to regret something *etwas noch bereuen* **A:** be sorry later for what you've done **B:** In spite of father being out of work, you stole your mother's housekeeping money to buy a new CD. You'll live to regret that (one day).

RIDE

take someone for a ride *jemanden übers Ohr hauen, aufs Glatteis führen* **A:** cheat/swindle someone **B:** Watch out with open markets on your holiday in Southern Europe, don't accept the first price and inspect the products carefully, they like taking tourists for a ride.

SAFE

Better (to be) safe than sorry *Vorsicht ist besser als Nachsicht* **A:** better to be careful at the beginning rather than regret it later **B:** Your mother is already in bed with a cold, put on a thick coat before you go to the disco, better safe than sorry.

SAID

(It's) easier said than done *(Es ist) leichter gesagt als getan* **B:** On your way to the bank, could you return my books at the library. – That's easier said than done, I've got to go shopping and have an appointment with the dentist.

SAME

It's all the same to me *Das ist mir alles gleich, ist mir egal* **A:** I couldn't care either way **B:** It's all the same to me, whether we go to the supermarket round the corner or in the next village, they're as good as each either.

boil down to one/the same thing *auf dasselbe hinauslaufen* **A:** amount/come to the same thing

MIND – FEELING

B: Whether we reduce wages or reduce the number of workers, it boils down to the same thing, we have to cut personnel costs.

SCENT

throw someone off one's scent *jemandem von der Spur abbringen* **A:** throw someone off his track/path **B:** The escaped criminals threw the police dogs off their scent by leaving the forest and swimming down a river.

SENSE(S)

lose all sense of reason *von allen guten Geistern verlassen sein* **B:** When the USA and the UK declared war on Iraq in 2003, many people thought George Bush and Blair had lost all sense of reason.

That/something makes sense *Das klingt plausibel* **A:** seems plausible **B:** That makes sense what you said about the competitors, we should act immediately and reduce our prices as well.

be out of one's senses *nicht bei Sinnen sein, verrückt sein* **A:** take leave of one's senses **B:** You must be out of your senses, your 50th birthday is tomorrow, you can't phone 70 guests and say the party is off.

come to one's senses *zur Vernunft kommen* **A:** regain one's sanity **B:** You'll never get your pilot licence drinking all the time, if you want to fly then come to your senses, and quit alcohol immediately.

bring someone to his senses *jemanden zur Vernunft/Besinnung bringen* **A:** persuade someone to act reasonably **B:** When his wife opened the window, and hundreds of his precious stamps flew out, he went mad with anger, but she managed to bring him to his senses with a beautiful meal.

take leave of one's senses *den Verstand verlieren, seine fünf Sinne nicht beisammen haben* **A:** go off his mind **B:** The woman does drink a lot, but yesterday she must have taken leave of her senses, she was caught in a supermarket totally naked.

SHAME

be a crying shame *eine Schande sein* **A:** that's the very limit **B:** It's a crying shame when children are separated from one another, because their parents have divorced.

SIGHT

have (a) second sight *das zweite Gesicht haben, hellsehen können* **A:** have a second perception **B:** Your mother must have second sight, she cancelled her flight yesterday, sensing there would be an accident today, and I've just hear that the plane she booked crashed.

out of sight, out of mind *aus den Augen, aus dem Sinn* **A:** the longer one is away, the easier it is to forget **B:** You were always worried about your sick uncle for years. – Well, he suddenly left for a world cruise 4 months ago, out of sight out of mind.

SLOW

(be) slow but sure *langsam aber sicher* **V:** (do something) slowly but surely **B:** Well he's not the quickest book-keeper we've had, but he's slow and sure, and accuracy is important.

SORROWS

drown one's sorrows *Kummer im Alkohol ertränken* **A:** drink to forget (also in general: try to forget one's worries by a holiday, theatre etc.) **B:** After his wife suddenly left him, he was drowning his sorrows in the local pub for weeks.

STEAM

work/let off steam *Dampf ablassen* **A:** get it out of one's system **B:** One advantage with boarding schools, is after the lessons the pupils can work off steam with sports in the afternoons.

SWOOP

do something in one fell swoop *auf einen Schlag, in einem Griff* **A:** at the stroke of his hand **B:** The new owner didn't waste time with re-structuring his company, he changed the firm's management in one fell swoop.

TETHER

be at the end of his tether *am Ende seiner Kraft sein* **A:** be at an end **B:** He was at the end of his tether after receiving bad news three times within one day.

THICK

stick/stay together through thick and thin *zusammen durch dick und dünn gehen, zusammenhal-

MIND – FEELING

ten wie Pech und Schwefel **A:** hold out together **B:** I've always said, getting married is no problem, but sticking together through thick and thin is the real test of a relationship.

THING

not know the first thing about something *von Tuten und Blasen keine Ahnung haben* **A:** not have a clue **B:** I'd love to help you typing data into your files, but I don't know the first thing about computers.

THOUGHTS

have second thoughts about *Zweifel haben an* **A:** have doubts about **B:** The job paid well, but he had second thoughts about the location, 3 years in the tropical jungle could be dangerous.

TOP

something gets on top of someone *jemandem wachsen die Dinge über den Kopf* **A:** cannot cope with it **B:** I'll have to speak to our neighbour, he's practicing on his piano in the afternoons and well into the night, and it's getting on top of me.

go over the top *zu weit gehen, überreagieren* **A:** act spontaneously/rashly **B:** Although she only had 30 euros to spend, when she saw a painting of her favourite artist, she went over the top and bid 100 euros for it.

TUNE

call the tune *Wer zahlt hat zu bestimmen* **A:** have the last word **B:** Persuading your father that you come with us on a skiing holiday, could be difficult; as long as you're studying and not earning, he calls the tune.

TURN

One good turn deserves another *Eine Hand wäscht die andere* **A:** we'll make ourselve quit **B:** Jack took my wife to hospital, when my car was being repaired, and I looked after his dog, when he was on holiday, one good turn deserves another.

UPTAKE

be quick/slow on the uptake *schnell/langsam von Begriff sein* **A:** quick/slow at understanding **B:** I kept pointing to my watch to show him we'll miss the train if we don't move now, and he continued reading, he's (a bit) slow on the uptake, isn't he?

USE AGAINST

use something against someone *jemandem einen Strick aus etwas drehen* **A:** turn the facts round **B:** The school director's understanding towards youths taking drugs soon ceased, when he realised the press could use it against him.

WASTE

waste not, want not *Spare in der Zeit, so hast du in der Not* **A:** extravagance leads to poverty, save something for a rainy day **B:** Why throw all your clothes out, they still fit you and we can save money, waste not, want not.

WAY

look the other way *ein Auge zudrücken, wegschauen* **A:** turn a blind eye **B:** The referee was very fair, when he saw the young lad accidentally touch the football with his hand, he looked the other way.

go out of one's way to *sich besondere Mühe geben/keine Mühen scheuen* **A:** put oneself out to **B:** When we visited Germany, our friends went out of their way to show us their city and make our stay so enjoyable.

find (something) out the hard way *aus dem eigenen Schaden lernen/klug werden* **A:** learn the hard way **B:** We said you should have bought a car and not a motor bike; after your third accident in a month you've found (it) out the hard way.

bring/take/put him out of harm's way *in Sicherheit bringen/stellen* **A:** in a safe place **B:** The older boys are playing with stones, I'd take your brother to another playground and bring him out of harm's way.

pave the way for *jemandem den Weg ebnen* **V:** clear the way for **A:** create/give room for **B:** The first landing on the moon paved the way for future aeronautical developments.

go about something the wrong way *falsch zu Werke gehen, verkehrten Ansatz einsetzen* **A:** take/use the wrong approach **B:** No wonder your boss didn't support your new project, you went about it the wrong way by

MIND – FEELING

insulting him at the meeting in front of our best customer.

not know which way to turn *nicht wissen, wohin (man sich wenden soll)* **A:** be sixies and sevens **B:** During my holiday in Saudi Arabia, my car broke down miles from the nearest city; I didn't know which way to turn, until a police car appeared and helped me out.

not have it both ways *Beides kann man nicht haben* **A:** not have both ends of the stick **B:** George, you can have a risky investment with high interest or a secure one with low interest, but you can't have it both ways.

there are no two ways about it *Es führt kein Weg daran vorbei* **A:** there is no other possibility **B:** When you're in the army, you'll have to obey orders however unreasonable they seem; there are no two ways about it.

WELL

All is well that ends well *Ende gut, alles gut* **B:** First our car didn't start, then the taxi didn't arrive, and if it weren't for our neighbour, we would have been late for the theatre – well as they say „All's well that ends well."

WISE(R)

put someone wise to *jemanden über jemanden/etwas aufklären* **A:** make someone aware of **B:** Since joining our school, you're very popular with our teaching colleagues, but I'd like to put you wise to the opinion of the director on your teaching methods.

be wise(r) after the event *Hinterher ist man immer schlauer* **A:** everyone can say that afterwards **B:** We should have driven quicker, the train left 2 minutes earlier than expected. – Well, we couldn't have known that, besides one is always wise after the event.

be none the wiser *So klug wie zuvor* **A:** not understand anymore than I did before **B:** Sorry George, you've spent an hour explaining your problem, but I'm none the wiser; if you want me to help you, you'll have to explain it better.

WITS

have one's wits about one *seine Gedanken beisammen haben/ei-*

nen klaren Kopf haben **A:** keep his wits about him **B:** When he swam out too far and was pulled by the strong current, he had his wits about him and carefully directed himself towards the end of the jetty.

frighten the wits out of someone *jemanden einen Todesschrecken einjagen* **A:** frighten the living daylights out of someone **B:** Four weeks after my mother had died, my wife tried on one of my mother's dresses, when I saw my wife in the dimly lighted hall, she frightened the wits out of me.

drive someone out of his wits *jemanden um seinen Verstand bringen* **A:** drive someone mad/insane/crazy **B:** A day before the removal van came, my wife drove me out my wits by opening four boxes and cleaning all the silver.

be out of one's wits *verrückt sein, den Verstand verloren haben* **A:** be out of his senses or mind **B:** Jack has had one week's sailing course, and he's now going to sail across the Atlantic in a yacht by himself. He must be out of his wits.

be at one's wits' end *mit seinem Latein/seiner Weisheit am Ende sein* **A:** be in total despair **B:** Her father died two days ago, and her mother was rushed to hospital yesterday with a suspected brain tumour, she must be at her wits' end.

WRONG

get (hold of) the wrong end of the stick *etwas völlig missdeuten/falsch verstehen* **A:** get it round the wrong way **B:** You've got the wrong end of the stick, Jack, your wife gave me a hug when I told her my father had died yesterday, there's no need to begin divorce proceedings.

get out of bed on the wrong side *mit dem linken Fuß aufstehen* **A:** be irritable or bad-tempered **B:** Since he came into the office today, he's been moaning at everyone. He must have got out of the bed on the wrong side this morning.

CHARACTER

ABREAST
keep abreast (of things) *auf dem Laufenden bleiben* **A:** keep on the ball **B:** He's the best doctor in town, he always has time for his patients and keeps abreast of changes in treatment methods and pharmaceutical products.

AHEAD
be ahead (of others) *die Nase vorn haben* **A:** be in front **B:** Just before the end of the season, Manchester United were ahead of the other clubs by 10 points.

be ahead of one's time *seiner Zeit voraus sein* **V:** be born ahead of one's time **A:** be before his time **B:** Leonardo de Vinci was ahead of his time, he designed aircrafts and a bicycle years before they were invented.

BOLD
be (as) bold as brass *frech wie Oskar, unverschämt sein* **A:** not have any scruples **B:** I gave your daughter some money for sweets, then she stuck her tongue out as bold as brass and ran away.

COURAGE
have the courage of one's convictions *Zivilcourage haben* **A:** stand/stick up to/for one's principles **B:** I'm not sure, if taking 30 dogs into the supermarket as a protest against cruelty to animals, achieves your purpose, but I respect you for having the courage of your convictions.

COLOURS
show his true colours *sein wahres Gesicht zeigen* **A:** show his true self **B:** My brother showed his true colours, when he learnt he hadn't been mentioned in father's last will, he burnt the parent's house to ashes and disappeared.

COLD
be as cold as ice *eiskalt sein* **A:** be freezing **B:** I'd stay in today after that heavy cold, your mother just came in from shopping and her hands and ears were cold as ice.

DARK
keep someone in the dark *jemanden über etwas im Dunkeln lassen* **A:** conceal the truth from someone **B:** Many assume that the dictator of Iraq with respect

to atomic weapons has kept the UN inspectors so far in the dark.

ENVY

be eaten up with envy *vor Neid aufgefressen werden* **A:** be green with envy be full of envy/jealously **B:** We'd been close friends for years, but after I'd inherited a lot of money, he was eaten up with envy and our relationship ended.

EXHIBITION

make an exhibition of oneself *sich lächerlich/zum Gespött machen* **A:** ridicule onself **B:** It's embarrassing going out for dinner with George, he always makes an exhibition of himself by shouting or whistling at the waiters.

INSULT

add insult to injury *alles noch schlimmer machen* **A:** aggravate someone even more **B:** Your poor wife burnt her fingers badly while preparing the dinner for 3 hours, then you added insult to injury, by telling her the meal tasted awful.

LAURELS

rest on one's laurels *sich auf seinen Lorbeeren ausruhen* **A:** be content with past achievements **B:** That star footballer should be careful. After being elected Footballer of the year, he has slackened off with his training, he shouldn't rest on his laurels.

LOT

be a bad lot *ein übler Bursche, mieser Typ sein* **A:** be an ugly customer **B:** He's always stealing money from people, he's a bad lot.

MARTYR

make a martyr of oneself *(satirisch) sich aufopfern, den Märtyrer spielen* **A:** play the martyr **B:** I've laid the table, cooked the meal, and washed up, do you think you could dry up the dishes. – Don't make a martyr of yourself, you know I always do the drying up.

MIND

have a one-track mind *nur das eine (eins) im Kopf/Sinn haben* **A:** be absorbed in a single topic **B:** After the date with Jack, Susan lost interest in him; it doesn't surprise me, he's got a one-track mind, he only thinks of sex.

CHARACTER

have an open mind (on/towards) *unvoreingenommen sein, offen für etwas sein* **A:** be open-minded **B:** I have an open mind on nationalities, I will decide at the interview whether the African candidate is suitable for the job or not.

have a mind of one's own *seinen eigenen Willen haben, wissen was man will* **A:** make one's own mind up **B:** There's no need to ask your mother what you should wear tonight, you're old enough to have a mind of your own, young lady.

PRINCIPLES

live up to one's principles *gemäß seinen Grundsätzen/nach seinen Prinzipien leben* **A:** live/act according to one's principles **B:** After his divorce, he vowed he would never marry again; he lived up to his principles, when his new partner insisted on marriage after 10 years, he ended the relationship.

REPUTATION

live up to one's reputation *seinem Ruf gerecht werden* **A:** live up to one's expectations **B:** We've heard the new Headmaster is very strict. – Well, he's certainly living up to his reputation; he's already suspended 4 youths for smoking in the school.

TOWER

be/live in an ivory tower *in einem Elfenbeinturm sitzen/leben* **A:** live in a dream house **B:** Studying business at University is like living in an ivory tower, when you enter the real business world, you might be shocked.

WAY

have a way with someone *mit jemandem gut umgehen können* **A:** have that certain something with **B:** She certainly has a way with children, they were polite and helpful, although the previous teacher told her the pupils were very rude.

have one's own way *seinen Willen durchsetzen* **A:** insist on doing what he wants **B:** His mother adores him so much, he always has his own way; he's lucky his father doesn't know what his son gets away with.

be set in one's ways *in seinen Gewohnheiten festgefahren sein*

A: be set in one's habits, attitude **B:** You can forget inviting the older members of staff to the computer seminar, they are too set in their ways.

MONEY – FINANCE

ACCOUNT

give a good account of himself *eine gute Figur abgeben, sich gut schlagen* **A:** present oneself well **B:** In spite of his prison sentence, he gave a good account of himself at the interview and got the job.

BARGAIN

make the best of a bad bargain *gute Miene zum bösen Spiel machen* **A:** make the best of a bad job **B:** You lost the contract with the leading discount store here, make the best (out) of a bad bargain, and increase our exports to Eastern Europe.

drive a hard bargain *hart verhandeln, mächtig rangehen* **A:** make an offer on one's own terms/without making any concessions **B:** You're driving a hard bargain by offering me only 200 pounds for my old car, but I'll accept it, I need the money.

be a bargain at that price *für den Preis geschenkt sein* **A:** be very cheap **B:** I'd buy that leather jacket reduced by 50%, it's a bargain at that price.

CASH

cash in on something *seinen Vorteil daraus ziehen* **A:** take advantage of **B:** Being a midget, Ken had difficulty finding a job, until one day he cashed in on his abnormality by becoming a popular clown in the circus.

CROWN

to crown it all *als Krönung des Ganzen* **A:** to cap/top it all **B:** James won't fly again, his suitcase was 40 kg overweight, his plane was delayed 2 hours, and to crown it all, he couldn't find his passport on arrival.

DOLLAR

bet one's bottom dollar *Gift darauf nehmen können* **A:** put/bet one's last penny on it **B:** He hasn't got a chance against the

MONEY – FINANCE

other boxer, I'd bet my bottom dollar, that he won't win.

GOLD

be as good as gold *ein Schatz/Gold wert sein* **A:** be very well behaved **B:** Young Susan was with us for a fortnight, while her parents were on holiday, and was never a problem, she was good as gold.

worth his/its weight in gold *Gold wert sein, unschätzbar* **A:** can't/couldn't do without her/it **B:** Your new housekeeper is worth her weight in gold, does the cooking, cleaning and looks after your children like a nanny.

MINT

make/earn a mint *sich eine goldene Nase verdienen* **A:** make/earn a lot of money **B:** How did Peter afford such an expensive house? – He was very lucky, he made a mint on the stock exchange.

MONEY

put money away/aside *(Geld) auf die hohe Kante legen* **A:** put it away for a rainy day **B:** I wouldn't invest all that money you inherited in shares, I'd put some aside until you hear what the tax authorities want.

be money (thrown) down the drain *Geld aus dem Fenster geschmissen* **B:** Don't buy that expensive ski equipment, you know you never go skiing on holiday, that's money (thrown) down the drain.

put one's money where one's mouth is *Taten sprechen lassen* **A:** well you wanted to do it **B:** You wanted the diploma to improve your career, so don't sit here watching TV, put your money where your mouth is, and get off to night school.

money is no object *Geld spielt keine Rolle* **A:** money is no problem **B:** Our new villa in Spain is almost finished, darling; can you order the decorations and furniture, money is no object.

be rolling in money *in Geld schwimmen* **A:** have pots of money **B:** I told Jack that we can't go on holiday with them to the Bahamas, because I'm working; they forget we're not rolling in money as they are.

PENCE

take care of the pence and the pounds (will) take care of themselves *Spar im Kleinen, dann hast du im Großen; wer den Pfennig nicht ehrt, ist des Talers nicht wert* **A:** save a little and it soon mounts up **B:** Peter, why do take the bus to work instead of the taxi? – Well, my motto is: take care of the pence and the pounds take care of themselves.

PENNY

make an honest penny *sein Geld/Brot ehrlich verdienen* **A:** earn an honest living **B:** You've got the wrong impression about Jack, he may look like a tramp, but he makes an honest penny.

not have a penny on me *keinen Pfennig (in der Tasche) haben* **A:** to be skint/penniless **B:** I can't lend you any money, I haven't got a penny on me.

in for a penny/in for a pound *Wenn schon, denn schon/Wer A sagt, muss auch B sagen* **A:** go the whole stretch **B:** Don't give up now, we've done 3 of the 5 disciplines for the sport certificate, let's do the last two, in for a penny in for a pound.

a penny for your thoughts *etwas darum geben, jemandes Gedanken lesen zu können* **A:** what are you thinking about/of? **B:** You've been sitting here staring at the blue sky for the last two and a half hours, a penny for your thoughts.

(then) the penny dropped *der Groschen ist gefallen* **A:** grasp it in the end **B:** It was a mystery, how the neighbours suddenly bought a new house, two sports cars and a yacht, and then the penny dropped – they had won on the lottery!

haven't got a penny/cent to my name *völlig pleite sein, keinen Pfennig besitzen* **A:** haven't a penny on me **B:** When Jim saw the beggar stretch out his hand, he said to him: I'm out of work, I haven't got a penny to my name either.

RANSOM

pay or be (worth) a king's ransom *eine stolze Summe sein/bezahlen* **A:** pay/be worth a fortune **B:** You paid a king's ransom for that house, did you win the lottery?

MONEY – FINANCE

hold someone to ransom *jemanden erpressen* **A:** blackmail someone **B:** Before you can play football you must help your father in the garden; don't hold me to ransom, mum, I can help Dad tomorrow.

SCRAPE

scrape through *sich gerade so durchschlagen* **A:** just (about) get by, struggle through **B:** How are you getting on after changing jobs for less money? – We're scraping through alright.

WAY

pay one's way *auf eigenen Füßen stehen, für seinen Unterhalt selbst aufkommen* **A:** stand on one's own two feet **B:** Well he took a long time studying, but he's paying his way now in his first job; so we should be able to afford a holiday this year.

NAMES – NUMBERS

ALECK

smart alec(k) *Besserwisser* **A:** a know-all **B:** Jack's a smart aleck, he put new oil in my car, saying that was the problem, and the garage found that the filters were blocked.

BILLY

be a silly Billy *Dummerchen, Dummkopf, albern* **A:** be a bit stupid/silly **B:** You're a silly Billy, if you'd taken the letters to post when you went shopping, then you could have saved a second journey to the post office.

BOB

Bob's your uncle! *Fertig ist der Lack!* **A:** just like that **B:** John wanted the Director's position and after chatting with his uncle who owns the company he got the job, Bob's your uncle.

COUNT

Count me out/in! *Ohne mich!/ Da mache ich nicht mit!/Sie können mit mir rechnen* **A:** be all for it/dead against it **B:** We're forming a communist party, would you like to join! – Count me out! Our club has arranged a golfing holiday in Spain! – Count me in!

FIRST

first come first served *Wer zuerst kommt, mahlt zuerst* **B:** The flat is still free, but there are several people interested in it, I'd contact the agency now, first come, first served.

FORTY

have/take forty winks *ein Nickerchen machen* **A:** have/go for/take a nap **B:** After retirement, George was very active, but since reaching 70, he looks forward to having forty winks in the afternoon.

HALF

his/your/my better half *die bessere Hälfte (generally said by the husband)* **A:** pride of my life **B:** You haven't met my better half yet, she should be back in 10 minutes and I'll introduce you.

HALVES

not do something by halves *keine halben Sachen machen* **A:** not start something without finishing **B:** She doesn't do anything by halves, she does the house cleaning thoroughly until the whole house and contents sparkle.

go halves with someone *mit jemandem etwas teilen, halbe-halbe machen* **A:** split it between us **B:** George, for our student flat we need a new kettle, I haven't enough money, can you go halves with me?

HOBSON

have/be Hobson's choice *keine Wahl haben, friss oder stirb* **A:** have no choice at all **B:** When Henry Ford started producing cars, the Americans had Hobson's choice regarding the colour, because only black cars were offered.

JACK

I'm all right, Jack *Das juckt mich überhaupt nicht* **A:** Blow you, I'm alright **B:** Don't take the last two pieces of cake, Jim and Mary will be here in 5 minutes; that's their problem for being late, I'm all right, Jack.

JACK FROST

see Jack Frost/Jack Frost was here *der Frost, Winter* **A:** winter is here **B:** It must be cold outside, you can you see Jack Frost has been at the window panes.

JACK OF ALL TRADES

be a Jack of all trades (but master of none) *Hans Dampf in allen Gassen sein* **A:** can lend his hand to anything **B:** Peter mended our burst water pipe, is he any good at electrical work? – I should think so; he's a Jack of all trades.

JACK ROBINSON

Before one could say Jack Robinson *in null Komma nichts, im Nu* **A:** before you can count to ten **B:** George does anything for money; if you offer him 20 Euros to mow the lawn, he'll be in the garden before you can say Jack Robinson.

JEKYLL AND HYDE

be a Jekyll and Hyde *eine gespaltene Persönlichkeit haben* **A:** have a split personality **B:** Careful with the new manager, one day he's helpful and polite, then suddenly gets abusive and threatens to fire you, he's a real Jekyll and Hyde.

MICKEY

take the mick(e)y out of someone *auf den Arm/die Schippe nehmen* **A:** make fun out of someone **B:** Don't take the mickey out of me because of my hair and clothes, my daughter just wanted me to look younger.

NAME(S)

clear one's name *jemandes Unschuld beweisen* **A:** be acquitted of an accusation **B:** Jack's name was cleared, when the witness confirmed he was with Jack in the theatre at the time of the robbery.

drag his name through the mud *jemandes guten Namen in den Schmutz ziehen, jemanden öffentlich schlecht machen* **A:** ruin one's good reputation **B:** When the press found out about his connection with child pornography, they dragged his name through the mud.

make a name for oneself *sich einen Namen machen* **A:** make one's mark **B:** He finally made a name for himself as an author, when his third book became the best-seller in England and America.

have a good/bad name *einen guten/schlechten Ruf haben* **A:**

have a good/bad reputation **B:** If you're looking for a good restaurant, there's one round the corner which has a good name for quality and fair prices.

give someone a bad name *jemanden in Verruf bringen* **A:** harm someone's reputation/standing **B:** Jack, if you don't treat our best customers more politely, then you'll give our company a bad name.

call someone names *jemanden beschimpfen* **A:** insult someone by calling them everything under the sun **B:** Stop calling Aunty Jane names all the time, if she weren't so deaf she would be very upset.

NINE

nine times out of ten *so gut wie immer* **A:** in most cases, (far) more often than not **B:** You make weather forecasts as a living, how often are they correct? – With forecasts for the next day, we're right nine times out of ten.

NUMBER

tell someone any number of times *jemandem etwas zigmal/x-mal sagen* **A:** tell again and again **B:** I can see you've got cold again, I've told you any number of times to dress up warmly during winter.

one's days/hours are numbered *jemandes Tage/Stunden sind gezählt* **A:** have not long to go **B:** Has somebody upset him in the office? – Well, his days are numbered, he's unhappy about retiring next month after 40 years with the firm.

ONCE

once and for all *ein für allemal* **A:** for the last time **B:** That designer dress is far too expensive, once and for all, the answer is no, you'll have to choose another present for Christmas.

ONE

go back to square one *noch einmal von vorne anfangen* **A:** start from the beginning again **B:** Gentlemen, I'm afraid we've deviated from the original problem we wanted to solve, we'll have to go back to square one.

PUNCH

be (as) pleased as Punch (with oneself) *sich wie ein Schneekönig freuen* **A:** be over de-

NAMES – NUMBERS

lighted **B:** Our daughter was pleased as Punch, when her article was published in the national newspaper.

SIX(ES)

That's six of one and half a dozen of the other *Das ist Jacke wie Hose, dasselbe in Grün* **A:** no difference at all **B:** Shall we go to the pleasant Spanish restaurant here or to the cosy Italian one just round the corner for our discussion. That's six of one and half a dozen.

be at sixes and sevens *durcheinander sein* **A:** be in a twist **B:** He's at sixes and sevens, since his wife suddenly left him after 30 years of married bliss.

TOM

be a peeping Tom *Voyeur, Spanner* **A:** be peering at people **B:** Jack is a real peeping Tom, he was arrested in the woman's clothing department again, looking at women trying on new underwear.

TOM, DICK AND HARRY

any/every Tom, Dick and Harry *jeder x-beliebige/Hinz und Kunz* **A:** any nonentity **B:** I don't like your guest list for my 50th birthday, we can't invite any Tom, Dick and Harry, my business colleagues will be there.

TOMBOY

be a tomboy *ein Wildfang sein* **A:** she acts more like a boy **B:** Our son came back from school with a black eye, and said your daughter did it! – Well, she's a tomboy, your son shouldn't have picked a fight with her.

TWO

put two and two together *eins und eins zusammenzählen* **A:** draw the right/obvious conclusion **B:** I've understood your problem, but if you can't put two and two together, then you won't solve it.

two's company, three's a crowd *ein Dritter stört nur* **V:** two's company, three's none **B:** Mary, I was looking forward to having an Italian meal with just ourselves, why does your brother have to come – two's company, three's a crowd.

RELATION-SHIP

ADO
much ado about nothing *viel Lärm um nichts* **V:** much to do about nothing **A:** be a storm in a teacup **B:** Screaming that I must wear a tie and suit for my mother's 80th birthday is much ado about nothing, darling; my mother looks forward to seeing me not my clothes.

APRON-STRINGS
be tied to (his) mother's apron-strings *am Rockzipfel der Mutter hängen* **A:** be tied to the apron-strings **B:** Susan wants to marry John. She can forget it, in spite of two years in the army, he's still tied to his mother's apron-strings.

ASS
an ass of oneself *sich blamieren, sich lächerlich machen* **A:** behave in a ridiculous/stupid manner **B:** Jack made an ass of himself, when he tried to mow his lawn after the snowfall.

BABY
be left holding the baby *die Sache ausbaden müssen/den schwarzen Peter haben* **A:** leave someone to face the music or sort it out alone **B:** When the company was losing money, the boss and financial director suddenly disappeared and I was left holding the baby.

BARK
someone's bark is worse than his bite *Bellende Hunde beißen nicht* **A:** not be so threatening/angry as he pretends to be **B:** Uncle Tom does shout about the place, but there's no need to be scared, he's gentle at heart and his bark is worse than his bite.

BEAUTY
Beauty is in the eyes of the beholder *Schönheit liegt im Auge des Betrachters* **B:** What do think of his new girl-friend? – Well, I wouldn't touch her with a barge pole, but beauty is in the eyes of the beholder.

BOY
be the blue-eyed boy *jemandes Liebling sein* **A:** be the boss's darling **B:** John was the boss's blue-eyed boy, he was promoted to a senior executive within 6 months.

RELATIONSHIP

CIRCLE

go round/argue/talk in circles *in Kreisen reden, sich im Kreise drehen* **A:** argue in all directions **B:** We've just been going round in circles for the last hour, and still not reached a solution.

COAST

the coast is clear *die Luft ist rein* **V:** the path/way is clear **B:** The coast is clear, Jack, I'm climbing over the fence to get some apples, if someone comes, whistle twice.

COPYCAT

be a copycat *ein Nachahmer sein* **A:** imitate someone **B:** Fred carries his school satchel on his shoulder instead of on his back. He's just a copycat, he's seen John doing the same for months.

DECKS

clear the decks *klar Schiff machen/sich bereit machen* **A:** have to clear the table **B:** Remove all the posters from our previous project, we have to clear the decks for our next campaign.

DEEP END

throw someone in at the deep end *jemanden ins kalte Wasser werfen* **A:** let him learn the hard way **B:** I hope you're not letting him make the presentation, he only been with us 3 months – if we throw him in at the deep end, he'll learn more quickly.

dive/plunge in at the deep end *sich kopfüber in eine Sache stürzen* **A:** go head first into something **B:** Our young lawyer dived in at the deep end insisting on defending our client; it was one of most difficult cases we've had, and he was lucky to win it.

FAMILY

be in the family way *schwanger sein, guter Hoffnung* **A:** be pregnant **B:** We'll have to cancel our holiday, Susan is in the family way and the birth is expected in the same month we planned to fly to Asia.

FATHER

like father, like son *wie der Vater, so der Sohn* **A:** he (son) is a chip off the old block (father) **B:** John always gets annoyed when things aren't running smoothly, in fact he reminds me of his father. – Well, you know the saying, like father, like son.

FLOP

be a (total) flop *ein Schlag ins Wasser sein* **A:** be for nothing **B:** The police raid on the drug dealers in the city park was a total flop, the dealers had been warned beforehand, and were already abroad.

GLANCE

at first glance *auf den ersten Blick* **A:** to all appearances **B:** At first glance, it looks as if the other driver caused the accident, but wait until the police come, they could establish that you were driving too quickly.

at second glance *auf den zweiten Blick* **A:** after looking again/more closely **B:** I thought that was my mother crossing the street, but at second glance the woman was far too young.

IMAGE

be the (very) image of someone *jemandem wie aus dem Gesicht geschnitten sein, wie er leibt und lebt* **A:** be the split(ting)/living image of him **B:** When Jack was younger he didn't resemble his father at all, but he's now the image of his father.

INNOCENT

as innocent as a new born child/babe/lamb *unschuldig wie ein (neugeborenes) Lamm* **V:** innocent as a newly born child/etc **B:** She certainly fooled me, she's been our neighbour for 5 years and acted as innocent as a newborn child, and now she's murdered her husband.

JOKE/JOKING

be a corny joke *schwacher/alter Witz* **A:** a weak or bad joke **B:** That's a corny joke, Jack, you've told that one at least 10 times before.

Joking apart *Spaß beiseite* **A:** look at it seriuosly **B:** We should sack the entire top management and take over the company ourselves. But joking apart, we should improve our efficiency and support top management better.

LEAGUE

be in league with someone *mit jemandem unter einer Decke stecken* **A:** be hand in glove with someone **B:** As a large sum of money disappeared from the company's balance, the police were sure that the Director was in league with his book-keeper.

RELATIONSHIP

POP

pop in (and/for) *auf einen Sprung (vorbei) kommen* **A:** drop in **B:** If you're driving through our village tomorrow, then pop in and see us. If you're in the neighbourhood pop in for a cup of tea.

PUT OFF

put something off *auf die lange Bank schieben* **A:** put it aside **B:** The wage dispute between Unions and government is so important, they should reach an agreement now, and not put it off for later.

SAFE

arrive safe and sound *gesund und munter ankommen* **A:** arrive in one piece **B:** After hearing there was snow and ice on the motorways, she was happy when her husband arrived home safe and sound.

SHIP

leave/abandon the sinking ship *das sinkende Schiff verlassen* **V:** like rats leaving the sinking ship **A:** abandon ship **B:** Typical of our finance manager, the company is losing money quickly, and just when we needed him he left the sinking ship and resigned.

something is (all) shipshape *in Ordnung, tipptopp* **A:** (thing) everything is ready **B:** You've prepared the meal and I've cleaned the flat up, so it's all shipshape for our guests.

SPICK

be (look) spick and span *(Sache) blitzsauber sein, (Person) wie aus dem Ei gepellt* **A:** (thing) be shipshape/spotless, (person) be perfect **B:** If your room is not spick and span before 6 o'clock this evening, you won't go to the cinema.

SQUARE

get square with someone *mit jemandem abrechnen* **A:** get quits with someone **B:** He beat me last year in the tennis final, this year I'm determined to get square with him.

STOPS

pull out all the stops *alle Hebel in Bewegung setzen* **A:** do everything in one's power **B:** For his wife's expensive operation, he pulled out all the stops to raise the money.

TALE

be an old wive's tale *ein Ammenmärchen* **V:** wife's or wives' tale **A:** downright lie **B:** Fred was visiting me to return the money I'd lent him, but he gave me an old wive's tale of a man robbing his money on his way to my house.

TERMS

be on good terms with someone *mit jemandem auf gutem Fuß stehen* **A:** be in someone's best books **B:** The new manager proved his knowledge and experience, within days he was on good terms with all members of staff.

THIEVES

be as thick as thieves *dicke/enge Freunde sein* **A:** be very close friends, stick together through thick and thin **B:** I wouldn't talk badly about John in front of Jim, they are as thick as thieves, and Jim will tell John everything.

TRIAL

learn something by trial and error *durch Versuch und Irrtum lernen* **A:** learn by trying everything out **B:** Many young people today have learned the computer by trial and error, rather than reading the manuals and attending courses.

WING

take someone under one's wing *jemanden unter seine Fittiche nehmen* **A:** give a person shelter/protection **B:** After Peter had lost his parents in a car crash, he was lost, but his grandmother took him under her wing.

WORDS

ABOUT

That's about it *Das ist wohl alles* **A:** that was it **B:** You said the robber came out of the bank with a suitcase and gun and drove away in a white van, did you see anything else? – No, that's about it.

be (just) about to do something *im Begriff sein etwas zu tun* **A:** in the same moment we wanted to **B:** We were just about to leave for a long walk in the fresh air, then the storm started.

ALL

all in all *unter dem Strich, alles in allem* **A:** in summary **B:** All in all, I was very satisfied with the final outcome of the negotiations.

ALONE

let alone *ganz zu schweigen von* **A:** not to mention **B:** Jack forgot our son's leg is in plaster; he wanted to take him for a bike ride, but our lad can't even walk, let alone ride a bike.

FANCY

(just) Fancy that! *Stellen Sie sich vor! Das gibt's doch nicht!* **A:** Would you believe it! **B:** When I saw the man in the see shouting for help, I swam out and brought him back to safety. – Fancy that, I thought you couldn't swim very well?

MAY

Be that as it may *wie dem auch sei* **A:** all the same **B:** I appreciate you couldn't get to work this morning because of your car accident; be that as it may, you'll have to stay in the office today until your report is finished.

TIP

tip of the iceberg *die Spitze des Eisbergs* **A:** be only the beginning **B:** In the corruption case the police arrested a minister, but added this is only the tip of the iceberg, there are other higher persons involved.

WAKE

in the wake of *als Folge von* **A:** as a (direct) consequence of **B:** In the wake of the bad local electoral results, the German Chancellor called for a general election in September.

WORD

the word is going around *es geht das Gerücht um* **A:** word has it, that… **B:** The word is going around, that Judy is pregnant and she doesn't know who the father is.

not get a word in edgeways/sideways *überhaupt nicht zu Wort kommen* **A:** talk with pausing for breath/to breathe **B:** When she starts talking, you'd just as well leave the room for an hour or two, you can't get a word in edgeways.

that's not the word for it *gar kein Ausdruck sein (für)* **A:** that's putting it midly **B:** You said the boss was impolite to me, that's not the word for it, he was bloody insulting.

take my word for it *Verlass dich drauf* **A:** believe someone is telling the truth **B:** He said he would pick us up at the station, but we've been waiting over an hour now; you shouldn't have taken his word for it – he's unreliable.

put in a good word for someone *ein gutes Wort für jemanden einlegen* **V:** say/mention a good word for **B:** I'm not too sure whether the boss thinks I'm suitable for the new position, could you put in a good word for me?

(right) from the word go *von Anfang an* **A:** (right) from the (very) start **B:** I'm not surprised he was fired, he's caused trouble in our company right from the word go.

be as good as one's word *sein Wort halten* **A:** keep to his promise **B:** I never thought Jack would baby-sit for us, but he was as good as his word and was at our door step at 7 p.m. on the dot.

must have/want the last word *das letzte Wort haben/behalten* **A:** 1) insist on being right 2) have the final decision/responsibiliy **B:** 1) Your second husband is as annoying as your first, he always has to have the last word in any discussion 2) Your idea is good, but you'll have to speak to the director, he has the last word in this matter.

a man of his word *ein Mann, der zu seinem Wort steht* **A:** he sticks to his word **B:** No need to doubt old Jim, he's a man of his word, if he told you he'll mend your car, he'll do it.

mum's the word *Aber kein Wort darüber, behalte es für Dich, nichts verraten* **A:** don't tell anyone else **B:** I've bought daddy's birthday present and hidden it under your bed, but mum's the word!

go back on one's word *sein Wort brechen* **A:** break one's word/ promise **B:** Her father had promised to go to her graduation party, but after his car accident he had to go back on his word.

WORDS

keep (to) one's word *sein Wort halten* **A:** keep one's promise **B:** Since I have to work when the removal van comes, your help is invaluable, so please keep your word, my wife can't manage it alone.

give someone one's word *sein (Ehren-)Wort geben* **A:** swear on it, that... **B:** You can't walk out on Mary, what about the kids? – I gave you my word that I'd leave, if she didn't change, here's my plane ticket.

man of few words *schweigsamer Mensch, nicht viel Worte machen* **A:** not say very much **B:** Did you think Philip enjoyed the party, he hardly opened his mouth all evening; well, he's a man of few words, but he rang this morning to thank us for a lovely time.

take the words out of someone's mouth *jemandem das Wort aus dem Mund nehmen* **A:** interrupt someone prematurely **B:** Excuse me for interrupting, I didn't want to take the words out of your mouth, but your reasons for being against the party are based on the false premises.

not mince one's words *kein Blatt vor den Mund nehmen* **A:** speak one's mind **B:** When the trade unionist heard the firm was putting 5000 workers off, he didn't mince his words when he met the management, accusing them of incompetence.

eat one's words *seine Worte zurücknehmen (müssen)* **A:** take back what he said **B:** My amateur club never thought much of my football skills, now they can eat their words, I start with Arsenal next season.

too (adjective e.g funnny) for words *unbeschreiblich komisch* **Note:** Used with most adjectives expressing feelings: too stupid, boring, ugly, easy etc. for words **A:** something is beyond words **B:** I'm sorry I laughed when you started your car in reverse gear, but when it jumped back knocking over the dustbin, it was too funny for words.

be lost for words *sprachlos sein* **A:** words fail me **B:** When the specialist told her, that her husband had only 3 months to live, she was lost for words.

VEGETATION

BUNCH

be the pick/best of the bunch *das Beste von allen sein* **A:** be the obvious/best/only choice **B:** There were 20 applicants, but he got the job – with his experience and qualifications, he was the pick of the bunch.

BUSH

beat about the bush *wie die Katze um den heißen Brei herumschleichen, um den heißen Brei herumreden* **A:** talk round the subject **B:** Don't beat about the bush, come to the point and admit the truth, that you're to blame for your marriage failing.

DAISY

be as fresh as a daisy *taufrisch/quicklebendig sein* **A:** full of energy **B:** After a relaxing holiday with regular sleep and good food, he returned to his job as fresh as a daisy.

HAY

hit the hay *sich in die Falle hauen, schlafen gehen* **A:** have a kip **B:** After such a hard day, I'm hitting the hay early tonight.

go haywire *durchdrehen* **A:** go berserk **B:** When his cat was run over, Jack went completely haywire, and smashed the driver's windscreen.

LEAF

shake like a leaf *zittern wie Espenlaub* **A:** shake all over **B:** When he heard his daughter had been rushed to hospital after a car accident, he was shaking like a leaf.

take a leaf out of his book *sich von jemandem eine Scheibe abschneiden* **A:** follow (from) his example **B:** Jack has been successfully self-employed for years, last week I took a leaf out of his book, quit my job and will start my own business next month.

turn over a new leaf *ein neues Leben anfangen, ein neues Kapitel aufschlagen* **A:** change one's way of life **B:** Jack was well known for being selfish, but after his wife survived a serious car accident, he turned over a new leaf, donating towards an association for disabled children.

VEGETATION

LOG

sleep like a log *schlafen wie ein Stein* **A:** sleep like a top **B:** After a 30 hour shift at the hospital, the head surgeon fell into his bed and slept like a log.

ROOT

that's where the root/crux of the matter lies *Da liegt der Hund begraben* **A:** that's the vital point/crux **B:** I can't take part in the sailing tournament, because my boat is in dire need of repair. I haven't got the money at the moment, and that's where the root of the problem lies.

ROSE

No rose without a thorn *Keine Rose ohne Dornen* **A:** every sweet has its sour **B:** Their new house was a dream, the surroundings were ideal, but their next door neighbours were unpleasant, no rose without a thorn.

STRAW

be the last straw *der Gipfel sein* **A:** that's the last straw **B:** You're the last straw, George, how on earth can you sell your house to buy a Ferrari sports car?

It's the (last) straw that breaks the camel's back *Das ist der Tropfen, der das Faß zum Überlaufen bringt* **A:** be the last small thing before the breaking point **B:** Jack has been sending rumours around the office about his boss. Yesterday he came 5 minutes late and his boss fired him on the spot, it's the last straw that breaks the camel's back.

TREE

bark up the wrong tree *auf dem falschen Dampfer/auf dem Holzweg sein* **A:** blame the wrong person **B:** Jack couldn't have taken your documents from your office desk, he was out all day, you're barking up the wrong tree.

WOOD

touch wood *auf Holz klopfen, viel Glück* **A:** as luck may have it, Nuance 2: Good luck **B:** Poor Jack will have to be operated again, because of his back problems. – I've thankfully never had problems with my back in my life, touch wood.

not see the wood for (the) trees *den Wald vor lauter Bäumen nicht sehen* **A:** not to see/identify the essential for too much detail **B:** His new book was full of so many characters, that I lost track of the actual plot to the story, I couldn't see the wood for the trees.

TIME – DAY

DAY

there is always another day *aufgeschoben ist nicht aufgehoben* **B:** Your brother rang to say he can't come to mend my bicycle this evening, don't worry, there's always another day.

call it a day *Feierabend machen* **A:** let's stop **B:** We've worked 10 hours today on repairing the roof, let's call it a day, we can continue tomorrow.

save something for a rainy day *etwas auf die hohe Kante legen* **V:** put something away for a rainy day **A:** put it aside for later/ the future **B:** You won so much on the lottery; I'd wouldn't spend it all, but save something for a rainy day.

make someone's day *jemandem den Tag retten/versüßen* **A:** make everything right/perfect **B:** Susan hadn't heard from her daughter for 6 months, then the daughter suddenly phoned from Australia, that made Susan's day.

DAYLIGHT

in broad daylight *am helllichten Tage* **A:** right in front of everybody **B:** Unbelievable, the old lady was robbed in the middle of the town in broad daylight.

scare/frighten the daylights out of someone *jemanden zu Tode erschrecken* **V:** living daylights **A:** scare/terrify someone to death **B:** When I complained about the tough meat in a French restaurant, the cook came out of the kitchen with a huge knife in his hand, he scared the (living) daylights out of me.

MONTH

not in a month of Sundays *Nie im Leben* **A:** not for donkey's years **B:** Jack promised to paint our garden fence in the next day or two. – You know old forgetful Jack, the fence will not be ready in a month of Sundays.

TIME

live on borrowed time *seine Uhr ist abgelaufen, seine Tage sind gezählt* **A:** time is against him **B:** John's cancer has spread from his stomach to his liver and kidneys, the doctors give him maximum 6 months; in short, he's living on borrowed time.

make up for lost time *verlorene Zeit einholen/gutmachen* **A:** compensate for lost time **B:** I'm sorry you were ill for 3 days, but we need your report urgently, you'll have to make up for lost time by working evenings.

in the nick of time *gerade zur rechten Zeit, gerade noch (rechtzeitig)* **A:** in the very last last moment **B:** In spite of the taxi arriving 30 minutes late, they managed to reach the airport in the nick of time, 10 minutes before take-off.

Once upon a time *Es war einmal* **A:** a long (long) time ago **B:** Once upon a time, there were three little bears ...

time heals all wounds *Die Zeit heilt alle Wunden* **A:** with time, every pain or wound will heal **B:** The second world war has still not been forgotten, but time heals all wounds, and the younger generations in Europe are growing up without the burden of the past.

bide one's time *den rechten Augenblick abwarten* **A:** wait for the right moment **B:** He knew the Indians only attacked at night, so he kept in his hiding place, biding his time till sunrise.

kill time *die Zeit totschlagen* **A:** spend the time by doing something **B:** We had an hour's wait for the train, so to kill (the) time, we played cards.

TOMORROW

tomorrow is another day *Morgen ist auch noch ein Tag* **A:** there's always (a) tomorrow **B:** In spite of working 10 hours, we won't finish the garden today, but tomorrow is another day.

YEARS

not seen someone for donkey's years *ewig nicht gesehen* **V:** for donkey's ears **A:** not for a very long time **B:** You must have been ill or on holiday for a long time, Jack, I haven't seen you for donkey's years.

TOOLS

HOOK

let someone off the hook *jemandem etwas erlassen, davon kommen lassen* **A:** let someone off **B:** Come on Mary, he apologised for being late, there's no need to be angry still, let him off the hook and we can enjoy the evening.

JAM

get someone out of a/the jam *jemandem aus der Klemme helfen* **A:** help someone out of a tight spot **B:** When the firemen reached the wrecked car, they consoled the trapped driver, by saying they'd soon get him out of the jam.

be in a (real/right) jam *in der Klemme/Patsche sitzen/sein* **A:** be in a (tight) spot **B:** Jack was in a jam yesterday, his car broke down, he missed his doctor's appointment, and his kids had to be taken home from school in a taxi.

KEY

keep/put something under lock and key *hinter Schloss und Riegel halten* **A:** put it in a safe/secure place **B:** Before you go on holiday, I'd take that valuable painting from the wall and keep it under lock and key till you return.

NAIL

be a nail on one's coffin *ein Nagel zu jemandes Sarg sein* **A:** someone will be the death of me **B:** If the press find out the minister has been having an affair with a prostitute, that will be a nail on his coffin.

hit the nail on the head *den Nagel auf den Kopf treffen* **A:** find exactly the right answer **B:** After discussing for 2 hours on a solution to the problem of diminishing profits, the marketing director hit the nail on the head: „Reduce our wide product range down to profitable products."

(as) hard as nails *hart wie Stahl, knallhart* **A:** strong as an ox **B:** I wouldn't pick a fight with Jack, because he insulted you, he was a merchant soldier for years and is hard as nails.

SCREW

screw up one's courage *seinen ganzen Mut zusammennehmen* **A:** pull his strength together

TOOLS

B: It's difficult, leaving wife and kids to work for us in the middle of Africa for a year, but if you want to get on in our firm, then you'll have to screw up your courage, and go.

SPADE

call a spade a spade *die Dinge/das Kind beim (rechten) Namen nennen* **A:** be blunt to the point **B:** Our marriage was in a bad phase and my wife never understood me. – Why don't you call a spade a spade, and admit you had an affair with another woman.

SPANNER

put/throw a spanner in the works *einen Knüppel zwischen die Beine werfen* **A:** put a spoke in someone's wheel **B:** You threw a spanner in the works by telling the boss that George doesn't think much of the company, the boss wanted to promote George.

TOOLS

down tools *die Arbeit einstellen/streiken* **A:** stop working, go on strike **B:** When the Unions lost the argument for the wage increase, the workers downed tools.

WEDGE

the thin end of the wedge *es ist nur der Anfang/erster Schritt, so fängt's ja immer an* **A:** that's how it always goes **B:** Our business is going badly, if we allow a 5% wage increase now, imagine what the workers will demand when business improves! – Exactly, it's the thin end of the wedge.

TOWN – COUNTRY

BAR

prop up the bar *in der Kneipe hocken* **A:** be drinking (again) **B:** Where's your boozing uncle Sam? – He's propping up the bar as usual.

BRIDGE

that's all water under the bridge *das ist (alles) Schnee von gestern* **A:** that's dead/past and gone **B:** There's no point being sorry about your wife divorcing you, that's all water under the bridge, she remarried last week and went to live in America.

TOWN – COUNTRY

much water has flowed under the bridge *Seitdem ist viel Wasser den Rhein/den Fluß hinuntergeflossen* **B:** I wrote to our Professor after 25 years, he replied saying he had retired; no surprise, much water has flowed under the bridge since our student days.

cross one's bridges before one comes to them *Lassen wir es mal auf uns zukommen* **V:** cross that bridge when one comes to it **A:** worry about something that may never happen **B:** I know your wife's operation is critical, but stop thinking of the worst already, you're crossing your bridges before you come to them.

CORNER

be in a tight corner *in der Klemme/Patsche sitzen/sein* **A:** be cornered **B:** He's in a tight corner now, his wife and the woman he's been having an affair with accidentally met, and they're having a coffee together today.

DEAL

be (have) a raw deal *ein schlechter Handel* **A:** be an unfair deal **B:** 20 years with that chemical company and ruining your lungs, that was a raw deal getting only 500 Euros compensation.

DRIVER

be a backseat driver *schlechter Beifahrer* **B:** Going in one car with Peter and Jill makes economic sense, but you'll regret not going in two cars, Jill is a backseat driver.

HILL

be over the hill 1) *über den Berg sein, die schlimmste Zeit hinter sich haben* 2) *die besten Jahre hinter sich haben* **A:** 1) have the worst behind him 2) be in the prime of his life **B:** 1) He's finally over the hill, he got the director's job he was counting on 2) Jack's not worrying about promotion anymore; he's over the hill and enjoying his work.

go downhill *bergab gehen* **A:** go down (and down) **B:** Since losing his job and wife, he's gone downhill; we've got to help him before the situation worsens.

be as old as the hills *uralt, steinalt* **A:** as old as my teeth and a bit older than my tongue **B:** That joke you told us is like my dear Grandfather, as old as the hills!

MILLSTONE

be/carry a millstone round one's neck *ein Klotz am Bein sein* **A:** be great burden for **B:** Our son is 35 and still hasn't found a job, he's financially been a millstone round our necks for years.

MOUNTAIN

make a mountain out of a molehill *aus einer Mücke einen Elefanten machen* **A:** make more out of something than it really is **B:** There's no need to make a mountain out of a molehill, and cancel our holiday because the airlines are on strike, it only takes a few hours by train from London to Edinburgh.

NEEDLE

look for a needle in a haystack *eine Stecknadel im Heuhaufen suchen* **A:** look for/try to find something impossible (or virtually hopeless) **B:** Alex is on holiday, but we urgently need her report on the Smith affair, can you check in her office? – Forget it, in that disorderly mess, it will be like looking for a needle in a haystack.

ROAD

have one for the road *die letzte Runde trinken (in einer Kneipe/Party)* **A:** have the last round (of drinks) **B:** Come on David, we only celebrate your birthday once a year, let's have one for the road.

ROBBERY

be a daylight robbery *Wucher/Halsabschneiderei sein* **A:** be far too expensive **B:** That was a daylight robbery what the garage charged you for your car repair, my brother could have done it for a quarter of the price.

ROOST

rule the roost *der Herr im Haus sein* **A:** dominate **B:** When the owner's son started with the company, he was helpful and polite to his fellow workers, but when his father died, he changed and ruled the roost.

STREET

the man in the street *Durchschnittsbürger, Otto Normalverbraucher* **A:** average or ordinary person **B:** Your lecture on neurology was directed towards the medical profession and not the man in the street; I had difficulty following it.

not be in the same street as *nicht zu vergleichen mit* **A:** be far inferior to **B:** Well, if you insist on a game of tennis, then don't expect very much from me, you know I'm not in the same street as you.

go on the streets *auf den Strich gehen* **A:** walk the streets **B:** After she losing her job for the fourth time, the only alternative she saw was, to go on the streets again.

be streets ahead of someone *jemandem weit/haushoch überlegen sein* **A:** be head and shoulders above him **B:** The Japanese have been streets ahead of the Europeans in electronics and computer technology, but recently the gap has been closing.

TOWN

paint the town red *auf die Pauke hauen* **A:** celebrate excessively **B:** Lads, I won a million on the Lottery, tonight we'll paint the town red.

be the talk of the town *Stadtgespräch sein* **A:** (person) be the toast of the town **B:** After marrying the millionaire and throwing wild parties, she soon became the talk of the town.

TRACK

be on the track of someone *jemandem/etwas auf der Spur sein* **A:** be on the right path or trail of **B:** The researchers believe they are now on the (right) track to finding the causes for the disease.

lose track of someone/something *jemanden/etwas aus den Augen verlieren* **A:** 1) lose contact with someone 2) not able to follow the point, topic etc. **B:** 1) I last saw Jack 30 years ago, I've tried many times to find him, but I fear I've lost track of him forever 2) Peter, you've been talking so long, I've lost track of the original point!

be on the wrong/right track *auf der richtigen/falschen Spur sein* **A:** be on the right/wrong path or trail **B:** My father disappeared 20 years ago, but due to recent information I'm now on the right track, and should be able to find him soon.

lose (all) track of time *die Zeit vergessen* **A:** forget the time completely **B:** I was so engrossed in the book, that I lost (all) track of time, and missed my train!

TOWN – COUNTRY

stop dead in his tracks *abrupt stehen bleiben, plötzlich auf der Stelle stehen bleiben* **A:** suddenly freeze or remain motionless **B:** When a woman came out of the grocer's shop in the nude, Jack stopped dead in his tracks.

TRAIL

be hot on the trail of someone *jemandem dicht auf den Fersen sein* **A:** be very close to catching someone **B:** The police were hot on the trail of the bank robbers, when suddenly a helicopter landed in a clearing of the jungle, and flew off with the robbers.

WINDOW SHOPPING

be/go window shopping *einen Schaufensterbummel machen* **A:** have a look at the shops **B:** Our wives went into town this morning, but today's Sunday and the shops are shut; they're only window shopping.

WORLD – PLACES

CLOUD-CUCKOO-LAND

live in Cloud-cuckoo-land *in Wolkenkuckucksheim leben* **A:** live in an imaginitive unrealistic world **B:** You can't continue living in Cloud-cuckoo-land, you'll have to accept the problem as it is, and work out a realistic solution.

COVENTRY

send someone to Coventry *jemanden ignorieren, schneiden* **A:** leave someone out in the cold **B:** That was disloyal of you telling our competitors about our new research project, you were lucky the department didn't send you to Coventry.

DUTCH

be double Dutch to/for someone *für jemanden böhmische Dörfer sein, nur Bahnhof verstehen* **A:** it's all Greek to me **B:** It was nice of you to invite me to dinner with your new Italian friend, but you only spoke his language all evening, it was all double Dutch to me.

go Dutch *getrennte Kasse machen* **A:** each pays for himself **B:** There's no need to pay the bill for all of us, Jack, we're all still students, let's go Dutch.

Dutch courage *angetrunkener Mut* **A:** work up some courage with a few drinks **B:** Careful this evening, when you meet the fellow who hit your brother, he's an ex-boxer; then I'll order a double whiskey to give myself some Dutch courage.

be a Dutchman *Ich fresse einen Besen, wenn ...* **A:** then I can't believe a word you're saying **B:** If you're a brain surgeon, young lady, then I'm a Dutchman.

NEWCASTLE

take coals to Newcastle *Eulen nach Athen tragen* **A:** do something superfluous **B:** Giving him as a birthday present a book on the functions of the brain, is like taking coals to Newcastle; he's the top brain surgeon in the country.

PLACE

be/feel out of place *sich fehl am Platz fühlen/sein* **A:** like a fish out of water **B:** Susan had her best dress on at the party, but felt of place when she saw the other women in jeans and sport shoes.

put someone in his place *jemanden in seine Schranken weisen* **A:** pull him down an peg/inch or two **B:** The president suggested women's football would be more attractive, if they wore tighter shorts; a leading female player put him in his place, saying he should worry about the development of women's football instead of sex.

fall into place *alles/es macht plötzlich Sinn, sich zusammenfügen* **A:** make sense **B:** When I started the job, I didn't understand who was doing what, but after a few weeks everything fell into place.

take the place of *an die Stelle treten von jemandem, ihn ersetzen* **V:** take his place **A:** step in for **B:** You'll have to take the place of our leading violinist at tonight's concert, he's suddenly caught the flu (influenza).

put oneself in his place *sich in seine Lage/Stelle versetzen* **A:**

WORLD – PLACES

put oneself in his position **B:** That wasn't very loyal leaving the club and going to the Italian team; well put yourself in his place, he's been our substitute goal keeper for 3 years.

ROME

when in Rome, do as the Romans do *andere Länder, andere Sitten* **A:** adapt oneself to (the customs of) the country **B:** Gerd, the English girl at the next table is cutting the potatoes with her knife! – Getrud, we're in England, when in Rome, do as the Romans do.

All roads lead to Rome *Alle/Viele Wege führen nach Rom* **B:** Which direction is Frankfurt? Just keep driving, any direction will take you there, as they say – all roads lead to Rome.

WORLD

come up/down in the world *es zu etwas bringen bzw. herunterkommen* **A:** (come up) get on very well, raise his status (come down) lose his social/professional standing **B:** You've certainly come up in the world since our school days, I've heard you're President of your company.

be on top of the world *überglücklich sein* **A:** be in another world **B:** He never thought he's win 5 million on the lottery, since then he's been on top of the world.

be out of this world *phantastisch, himmlisch sein* **A:** be fantastic **B:** Just wait until you've heard his new song, we must buy it, it's out of this world.

It's not the end of the world *Davon geht die Welt nicht unter* **A:** things could get far worse **B:** There's no need to cry because you didn't get the job, it's not the end of the world, there are other firms looking for people like you.

Not for all the world *nicht um alles in der Welt, um keinen Preis* **A:** not for any price **B:** Wouldn't you like to leave your country cottage and return to the big city, where everything happens? – Not for all the world, I treasure my peace.

live/be in a world of one's own *in seiner eigenen (kleinen) Welt leben* **A:** live in a make-believe world (of her own) **B:** Susan didn't even recognise me today, she must be living in a world of her own again.

WORK – OCCUPATIONS

ACT

get in on the act *mit von der Partie* **A:** get into the act **B:** When our neighbours heard we were renting our spare room to a student, they got in on the act by building two rooms in their attic.

put on an act *Theater spielen* **A:** (just) put on a show **B:** David doesn't want breakfast and wants to stay in bed today because of a stomach ache. – Rubbish! He's just putting on an act, he has an exam at the school today.

BOOK

can read someone like a book *jemand ist wie ein offenes Buch* **A:** see through someone **B:** It's always the same with George, always needing money; whenever he appears smiling, you know what he'll ask for, you can read him like a book.

go(stick) by the book *sich an die Vorschriften halten* **A:** stick/keep to rules **B:** Our security man won't let you bring the champagne into the firm, even if you've become a father, he goes by the book.

be in someone's good/bad books *bei jemandem gut/schlecht angeschrieben sein* **V:** (bad) in his black books **A:** be in someone's favour/disfavour **B:** The boy was in the teacher's bad books after being disobedient. After spilling tea on her father's shirt, she washed his car and was in his good books again.

BUSINESS

make something one's (own) business *es sich zur (eigenen) Aufgabe machen* **A:** make it my (own) responsibly **B:** Sorry, but as his direct superior he hasn't followed your instructions, so I'm making it my business to see that he finishes the job on time.

WORK – OCCUPATIONS

mean business *es ernst meinen* **A:** be serious **B:** I wouldn't take the boss's speech so lightly, he means business, if profits don't increase by September, then people will lose their jobs.

CHAIR

chair the meeting *der Vorsitz einer Versammlung sein, den Vorsitz übernehmen* **A:** take the chair **B:** No need to worry about our discussion on Monday, Jack is chairing the meeting, and he's on our side.

CLUE

not have a clue *keinen Schimmer haben* **A:** not have the slighest/any idea **B:** I haven't got a clue why they gave me the job, I can't speak any foreign language.

COME-BACK

stage/make a come-back *Comeback machen* **B:** The singer was a big hit in the 60's, but as the oldies became popular again, he staged a come-back in the 90's and was very successful.

DONKEY-WORK

donkey-work *die Drecksarbeit* **A:** the hard, boring or unpleasant part of the work **B:** During our summer job as students, the regular factory workers gave us the donkey-work; cleaning the toilets and unloading the heavy machines from the lorry.

FIDDLE

be as fit as a fiddle *munter wie ein Fisch im Wasser, kerngesund sein* **A:** be fighting fit **B:** How's George after his operation? – I visited him yesterday, he was flirting already with the nurses in the hospital, he's as fit as a fiddle.

play (the) second fiddle to *die zweite Geige spielen* **A:** be the second choice **B:** You can understand the substitute goal keeper being happy about joining the World Cup team as number one, he's been playing the second fiddle to the keeper from Bayern for years.

be on the fiddle *krumme Dinger/faule Geschäfte machen* **A:** to fiddle **B:** Jack is either on the fiddle or he's won the lottery, otherwise he could never have afforded a world trip on a luxury liner.

FITS

work in fits and starts *sprunghaft, unregelmäßig arbeiten* **A:** work in spasms **B:** Do you think David would come to my party just before his final exams? – Possible, he works in fits and starts, and you might catch him on his day off!

JOB

give someone/thing up as a bad job *jemanden/etwas aufgeben* **A:** give it up as impossible **B:** After failing his driving test the third time, he gave it up as a bad job and kept to his bicycle.

make the best of a bad job *retten was zu retten ist, das Beste daraus machen* **A:** make the best of it **B:** He lost his job teaching English in Spain, and made the best of a bad job by washing dishes in a hotel kitchen; after a year his Spanish was brilliant.

That's just the job *Das ist genau das Richtige, ideal* **A:** That's exactly what's needed or wanted **B:** I can't get the wheel off with this thing, show me your tool box, give me the large spanner – that's just the job.

JUDGE

be (as) sober as a judge *stocknüchtern sein* **A:** be stonecold sober **B:** The newly trained pilot was caught drinking, and the captain reminded him that a pilot had to be sober as a judge 24 hours before take-off.

make a snap judgement *ein vorschnelles Urteil fällen* **A:** make a quick/hasty judgement or opinion on/about **B:** The Doctor explained to George, that he was cautious about making a snap judgement on the basis of his phone call, and advised him to make an appointment in the clinic.

JUSTICE

do someone justice *jemanden gerecht behandeln* **A:** treat/judge him fairly **B:** The police caught him without a safety belt, but did him justice by giving him a warning instead of a fine.

LAW

the long arm of the law *der lange Arm des Gesetzes* **A:** you can't escape the law **B:** Even if you rob the bank successfully, you won't escape; with international cooperation, it's difficult to avoid the long arm of the law.

WORK – OCCUPATIONS

keep on the right/wrong side of the law *sich (nicht) im Rahmen des Gesetzes bewegen* **A:** (right) keep straight **B:** When you leave prison next week, don't get up to your old habits of stealing again, but keep on the right side of the law.

loophole in the law *die Lücke des Gesetzes/Gesetzeslücke* **A:** a loose link in the chain **B:** As your lawyer, I must be honest and tell you, if we can't find a loophole in the law, then the chances of our winning the case are very small.

take the law into one's own hands *das Recht selbst in die Hand nehmen* **A:** follow his own laws **B:** During the pioneering days in America, law and order had not been properly organised and many took the law into their own hands.

lay down the law *ein Machtwort sprechen* **A:** tell someone where to get off **B:** I've told our two sons to stop fighting and go to sleep three times already, could you speak to them and lay down the law.

LIMELIGHT

be in the limelight *im Mittelpunkt stehen, im Rampenlicht stehen* **A:** steal the show **B:** After winning most of the medals on the school's sport day, he was in the limelight for some days, but then everyone soon forgot about it.

LINE

draw a/the line *die Grenze ziehen* **A:** set a limit (to one's tolerance) **B:** Jack has started drinking heavily since going to University, I drew the line at a couple of beers, but a bottle of whiskey each day is out of the question.

be the bottom line *unter dem Strich, das Entscheidende* **A:** be the basic point **B:** You've been talking around the problem for 15 minutes, but what's the bottom line, do we have to sell the company or not?

read between the lines *zwischen den Zeilen lessen* **A:** read what's behind it **B:** When I first started the book, I thought it was a comedy, but after reading between the lines, I realised it was a serious criticism against society.

MUSIC

be music to one's ears *Musik in jemandes Ohren sein* **A:** hear music in his ears **B:** Jack had been training for months, then the Olympic coach told him he would represent the country at the coming Olympic games, that was music to his ears.

face the music *die Suppe auslöffeln, die Folgen tragen* **A:** take the consquences **B:** The minister was solely responsible for having the factory built in a nature protected area, now he'll have to face the music.

PART

look the part (of) *auch so (danach) aussehen, die Rolle passt zu jemanden* **A:** resemble a particular role/type/person very well **B:** She hasn't finished her final medical exams yet, but I saw her in the hospital checking the patients and she certainly looked the part of the experienced doctor.

play the part of *die/seine Rolle spielen als* **A:** play the/his role of/as **B:** He played the part of the loving Grandfather very well, but he didn't fool me, he hates children.

play/take a part in *seinen Teil dazu beitragen, dabei helfen* **A:** contribute towards **B:** George played a/his part in restoring the old club house, he was delivering the cement every evening.

PRACTICE

practice makes perfect *Übung macht den Meister* **A:** get better the more you work at it **B:** I'v painted the kitchen walls. Well now you can paint the living room – practice makes perfect.

PRINT

read the small print *das Kleingedruckte lesen* **A:** watch out for hidden clauses and conditions **B:** Before you sign a contract, particularly with an insurance policy, it's always advisable to read the small print.

QUEUE

jump the queue *sich vordrängen* **A:** push yourself forward **B:** When you're waiting for a bus in England, you can't jump the queue; waiting in line is an English institution.

WORK – OCCUPATIONS

SCENE

come on(to) the scene *auftauchen/auf der Bildfläche erscheinen* **A**: appear out of the blue **B**: We'd already set the date for our marriage, then the new tennis trainer came onto the scene, and a week later she cancelled the marriage.

make a scene *jemandem eine Szene machen* **A**: kick up a fuss **B**: Come on Peter, don't make a scene now in front of everybody, he didn't spill his drink on your jacket on purpose, it was an accident.

have/need a change of scenery (scene) *Tapetenwechsel, Luftveränderung brauchen* **A**: need a change of air **B**: After working 6 months in the home for disabled people, you need a change of scenery, join me for a weekend at the sea.

be behind the scenes *hinter den Kulissen* **A**: out of public view **B**: Watching a world cup game is great, but what's happening behind the scenes makes it all possible, from medical support through to security people.

SHOP

talk shop *von seinem Fach reden, fachsimpeln* **A**: talk about one's specialised work/subject/area **B**: On bowling evenings, they both disturb the atmosphere by always talking shop. – Well, they're dentists and like to exchange views.

SHOW

steal the show *die Schau stehlen, im Mittelpunkt stehen* **A**: be in/steal the limelight **B**: One of the five area managers attending the crisis meeting stole the show by giving a brilliantly prepared presentation and a convincing solution to the problem.

give the (whole) show away *es/alles verraten* **A**: tell the whole story beforehand **B**: After buying a programme from America, the competing channel gave the show away, by saying who the murderer was in the final series.

run the show *den Laden schmeißen* **A**: be in charge **B**: I've got a complaint, the computer I bought doesn't work. – I'm only the assistant, you'll have to speak to the man over there, he runs the show here.

Trick

have a show-down with someone *sich mit jemandem auseinandersetzen* **A:** give someone what for **B:** I've warned that hooligan twice already that he should stop frightening my sister, it's time I had show-down with him.

SONG

go for a (mere) song *spottbillig/für ein Butterbrot zu haben sein* **A:** be dirt cheap **B:** It's a pity you didn't get to the sales early enough, that dress you wanted went for a song.

make a song and dance about it *sich über etwas übertrieben aufregen* **A:** over-react to something **B:** Father made a song and dance about their daughter coming home at 3 in the morning and his wife responded: but she's 21 years old and is no longer a child.

STAGE-FRIGHT

have stage-fright *Lampenfieber haben* **A:** have first-night nerves **B:** Even though the vicar prepared his sermons carefully, he always had stage-fright for a minute or two before starting his sermon.

TRADE

tricks of the trade *besondere Kunstgriffe, Geschäftskniffe* **A:** secrets of the trade/business **B:** Your business degree gave you the job, but now we have to go from theory into practice and teach you the tricks of the trade.

TRICK

know a trick/thing or two *wissen, wie der Hase läuft/etwas auf dem Kasten haben* **A:** she's not as stupid as you think **B:** How did your mother manage to make such a tasty meal out of what you burnt? – That's experience, she knows a thing or two.

that should/will do the trick *das müßte eigentlich hinhauen* **A:** that should settle/do it **B:** I've put some chewing gum over the puncture and pumped your tyre up, that should do the trick until we get home and can repair it properly.

How are tricks? *Was macht die Kunst? Wie geht's?* **A:** What's new? **B:** Haven't seen you for ages, how are tricks?

(the whole) bag of tricks *die (ganze) Trickkiste* **A:** his odds

WORK – OCCUPATIONS

and sods **B:** I don't know where the decorator has gone, but he must be back soon, he's left his whole bag of tricks in the kitchen.

WAY

work his way up from the bottom *von der Pike auf dienen, lernen* **A:** rise from the ranks **B:** It was no surprise that John, with no University degree, became board member at 40. He joined the firm at 16 and worked his way up from the bottom.

have come a long way *(inzwischen) sehr weit gekommen sein* **A:** climb the ladder (since then) **B:** You've come a long way since we last met; you were a flight attendant then, but I've heard you're now an airline pilot.

WORK

make light work of *damit spielend fertig werden* **A:** accomplish a job/task easily **B:** Let Robert mend your television, he does TV and other electrical repairs as a part time job, he'll make light work of it.

be/look a nasty piece of work *fies aussehen, ein übler Mensch sein* **A:** is/looks a dangerous one **B:** Have you seen Mary's new boy friend, he's a nasty piece of work, I wouldn't be seen dead with him.

It's all in a day's work *Das ist doch selbstverständlich* **A:** that's what we're here for **B:** Thanks for getting our daughter from school and reaching the hospital in time for the operation; the ambulance crew replied: That's all in a day's work.

have one's work cut out *alle Hände voll zu tun haben* **A:** be pushed to finish the job **B:** If he insists on getting married in June, then we'll have our work cut out getting the house ready in time for the wedding reception.

make short/quick work of *keine Zeit daran verschwenden, kurzen Prozess machen mit etwas* **A:** not waste any time with that **B:** Sorry I'm late, is there any pudding left? – I'm afraid the kids have eaten it all up! – Well, they certainly made short work of that!

give someone the works *1) jemanden in (durch) die Mangel*

WAR – WEAPONS

nehmen (drehen) 2) nach allen Regeln der Kunst (prächtig) verwöhnen **A:** 1) give him a right punch-up 2) treat him like a King **B:** 1) When I find the hooligan who beat my young brother, I'll give him the works **B:** 2) The night before his wedding we'll invite George out and give him the works.

WAR – WEAPONS

BATTLE

be half the battle *Damit ist schon viel/die Hälfte gewonnnen* **A:** that's half of the job/task (done) **B:** All the ingredients are prepared on the table and that's half the battle, now we just need to cook it all according to the recipe.

fight a losing battle *auf verlorenem Posten stehen/kämpfen* **A:** fight for a lost cause **B:** Our competitors have responded to our second price reduction, but we're fighting a losing battle, they have better financial resources than us.

fight the same battle *am selben/gleichen Strang ziehen* **A:** be in the same boat **B:** There's no point arguing about the possible causes, we're fighting the same battle, so let's concentrate together on a solution.

a battle-axe *der Drachen (für eine Frau)* **Note:** only applied to women **A:** a right dragon **B:** Jack's invited us for a meal, but his wife is a real battle-axe; telling her husband what to do all evening, and criticising him, but when she got aggressive, we left.

BOMB

go like a bomb *Bombengeschäft/-erfolg sein* **A:** be a sales hit **B:** Now winter is here, the fur-lined boots went like a bomb, we'll have to order some more.

cost a bomb *ein Vermögen/Schweinegeld kosten* **A:** cost a fortune **B:** Darling, normally your wishes are my command, but you can forget that Persian carpet, it costs a bomb.

CEREMONY

not stand on (any) ceremony *wenig Wert auf Etikette legen* **A:** not take something so formally/seriously **B:** We're terribly sorry, we overslept and your invitation was for 11 a.m. and it's now 2 p.m. – Don't worry, we don't stand on any ceremony, come round for a coffee.

DAGGERS

be at daggers with someone *mit jemandem auf Kriegsfuß stehen* **A:** be furious with someone **B:** Since Susan found out that her husband had had an affair with her friend Mary, she has been at daggers with Mary.

FIGHT

put up a good fight *sich tapfer zur Wehr setzen* **A:** do his best **B:** He didn't really have a chance of beating the school boxing champion, but he certainly put up a good fight.

have a fighting chance *eine faire Chance/Gewinnchance haben* **A:** have a resonable/fair chance **B:** David is still in a critical position after his operation, but he has a fighting chance of pulling through.

FORT

hold the fort *die Stellung halten* **A:** stay put (till I return) **B:** Susan, the painters are coming in an hour, but I have to go to the bank, can you hold the fort until I get back.

GUNS

be going great guns *voll in Schwung sein* **A:** be full of energy **B:** It's incredible at his age, but Grandfather is still going great guns, and his business gets better every day.

stick to one's guns *nicht weichen/nachgeben, festbleiben* **A:** stay steadfast **B:** The boss threatened him with early retirement if he didn't stop his criticisms, but he's sticking to his guns.

HATCHET

bury the hatchet *das Kriegsbeil begraben* **A:** make up **B:** We've been good friends since school, that was a stupid mistake having a short affair with your wife last year, can't we bury the hatchet and be good friends again?

KING

be fit for a king *geeignet/gut genug für einen König* **A:** a fit for a Queen **B:** That dinner you cooked was wonderful, it was fit for a king.

do something until kingdom come *bis in alle Ewigkeit weitermachen* **A:** do it until the cows come home **B:** Jack, you can try getting the wheel off your car until kingdom come; the wheel is rusted through and you haven't got the right tools.

LARGE

be (still) at large *auf freiem Fuß sein/frei herumlaufen* **A:** be running free **B:** After his escape from prison last week, the convict is still at large.

LOCK

lock, stock and barrel *mit Stumpf und Stiel/ganz und gar* **A:** everything **B:** You haven't paid the rent for 4 months, I want you out by tomorrow, together with all your possessions, lock, stock and barrel.

MATCH

be more than a match for someone *jemanden in die Tasche stecken/jemanden weit überlegen sein* **A:** be far more competent than someone **B:** After your 30 successful boxing fights, you have no need to worry about your young opponent, you're more than a match for him.

PUNCH-UP

have a punch-up with someone *mit jemandem eine Schlägerei haben* **A:** have a brawl/fight with someone **B:** I wouldn't go to the training club for a few weeks, after saying bad things about his father. – Jack is waiting to have a punch-up with you.

SCOT-FREE

let somone off scot-free *jemanden ungeschoren davonkommen lassen* **A:** not detain/accuse someone **B:** Well I thought he was the obvious suspect, but the police couldn't find enough evidence, so they let him off scot-free.

SHOT

like a shot *wie aus der Pistole geschossen, blitzschnell* **A:** at once **B:** If I were 30 years younger, I'd leave the country like a shot and make a career in Canada.

be a dead shot *unfehlbarer Schütze* **A:** be good marksman, sharpshooter **B:** The person who assassinated President Kennedy in the 60's in a moving car from such a distance, must have been a dead shot.

WAR – WEAPONS

be a shot in the arm (for) *eine Vitaminspritze* **A:** be a boost (up) or booster **B:** The discovery of oil in the North Sea was a shot in the arm for the British economy.

have a shot (at) *etwas (mal) versuchen/ausprobieren* **A:** have a go at **B:** You're a good tennis player, why don't you have a shot at squash during the winter months?

not by a long shot *bei weitem nicht* **A:** not by a long chalk **B:** Do you think you could survive an expedition to the North Pole this winter? – Not by a long shot, I lost a toe which froze on a skiing holiday.

STRUGGLE

be an uphill struggle *harter Kampf sein* **A:** be a struggle all the way **B:** It's an uphill struggle trying to teach Henry Latin, he can't even speak his own language properly.

TARGET

be a sitting target *leichte Beute sein* **A:** a sitting duck **B:** Politics is a sitting target for criticism from the press, and always will be.

TRAP

lay a trap for someone *eine Falle stellen* **A:** catch someone out **B:** The hunters laid a trap for the bear by digging a large hole covered with light sticks and grass and putting a piece of meat behind the hole.

TRIGGER

trigger off *auslösen, zur Folge haben* **A:** spark off **B:** The government fear that a big wage increase for the miners will trigger off similar wage demands from other industries.

WAR-PATH

be on the war-path *auf dem Kriegspfad sein* **A:** look for a fight **B:** You shouldn't have slapped his son in the face, the father is on the war-path now, so I hope you can defend yourself.

REGISTER

A

glatt wie ein **Aal** sein 16

jemanden **abblitzen** lassen 85

sich von etwas **ablenken** 106

ein **Ablenkungsmanöver** 18

ihm jemanden/etwas **abnehmen** 42

sich **abrackern** 22

von Tuten und Blasen keine **Ahnung** haben 114

Kummer im **Alkohol** ertränken 113

ganz **allein** dastehen, in einer gefährlichen Lage sein 93

ein für **allemal** 127

das ist wohl **alles** 133

alles darum geben 21

ein hohes **Alter** erreichen 95

ein **Ammenmärchen** 14

von **Anfang** an 135

es ist nur der **Anfang**/erster Schritt, so fängt's ja immer an 142

noch einmal von vorne **anfangen** 127

wie **angegossen** passen 60

sich um seine eigenen **Angelegenheiten** kümmern 106

angeschlagen sein 94

bei jemanden gut/schlecht **angeschrieben** sein 149

vor **Angst** zittern 62

per **Anhalter** fahren 56

jemanden zum **Anlehnen** haben 54

jemanden **anstacheln** 72

sich **anstrengen** etwas zu tun 107

sich vergeblich **anstrengen** 19

ein **Anteil** an etwas haben 83

die **Arbeit** einstellen, streiken 142

'n **Appel** und 'n Ei 15

zu Tode **arbeiten** 96

sprunghaft, unregelmäßig **arbeiten** 151

jemanden auf den **Arm**/auf die Schippe nehmen 126

jemanden mit offenen **Armen** empfangen 22

mit jemanden/es sich **arrangieren**/ auf etwas (scheinbar) eingehen 80

den **Ast** nicht absägen auf dem man sitzt 18

im selben **Atemzug** 101

(wieder) frei **atmen** können 13

leichte **Aufgabe**, klare Sache 83

jemanden/etwas **aufgeben** 151

Register

es ihm **aufbürden**, ihm zur Last legen 82

es sich zur (eigenen) **Aufgabe** machen 149

aufgeschoben ist nicht **aufgehoben** 139

aufgedonnert, aufgetakelt sein 60

jemanden über jemanden/ etwas **aufklären** 116

sich ins Nichts **auflösen**, spurlos verschwinden 66

sich nicht **aufregen** 62

sich über etwas übertrieben **aufregen** 155

einen Tag **Aufschub** geben, jemandem ein bißchen mehr Zeit lassen 97

etwas wie seinen **Augapfel** hüten 70

ein **Auge**/beide **Augen** zudrücken, wegschauen 28

jemandem ins **Auge** fallen 28

jemanden/etwas im **Auge** behalten 28

etwas im **Auge** haben, etwas tun im Hinblick auf 28

Auge in **Auge** gegenüberstehen 32

den Tatsachen ins **Auge** sehen 32

es springt direkt ins **Auge** 56

seine **Augen** nicht von jemandem/etwas lassen 28

hinten keine **Augen** im Kopf haben 28

jemanden/etwas mit anderen **Augen** sehen 28

nur **Augen** für einen/eine haben 29

Augen haben wie ein Luchs 29

keine **Augen** im Kopf haben 29

mit bloßem **Auge** erkennen 29

seinen **Augen** nicht trauen 29

etwas mit eigenen **Augen** sehen 29

die **Augen** offen halten 29

jemandem verliebte **Augen** machen 30

jemandem nicht in die **Augen** sehen können 30

die **Augen** vor etwas verschließen 30

die **Augen** sind größer als der Mund 30

sich die **Augen** ausweinen 30

jemandem die **Augen** auskratzen 30

jemandem die **Augen** öffnen 30

unter vier **Augen** 86

aus den **Augen**, aus dem Sinn 113

etwas mit verbunden **Augen** tun 32

(direkt) vor seinen **Augen** 53

jemandem/etwas aus den **Augen** verlieren 145

den rechten **Augenblick** abwarten 140

jemandem eine **Augenweide** sein 30

jemandem aus dem **Augenwinkel** betrachten 31

die Sache **ausbaden** müssen 129

etwas **ausbügeln**, ausgleichen, beseitigen 87

gar kein **Ausdruck** (für) 135

sich mit jemandem **auseinandersetzen** 155

sich total **ausgelaugt** fühlen 62

ausgepfiffen werden 13

auslösen, zur Folge haben 160

etwas **ausprobieren**, versuchen 39

eine faule **Ausrede** 103

auch so (danach) **aussehen**, die Rolle passt zu jemanden 153

einen gegen den anderen **ausspielen** 81

auswendig lernen 46

B

nur **Bahnhof** verstehen, für jemanden böhmische Dörfer sein 146

auf die lange **Bank** schieben 132

der Gedanke **bedrückt**/quält/ **beschäftigt** ihn 106

es ist nichts zu **befürchten**/ es ist sehr unwahrscheinlich, dass 104

im **Begriff** sein etwas zu tun 133

schnell/langsam von **Begriff** sein 114

für sich **behalten** 60

beides kann man nicht haben 116

schlechter **Beifahrer** 143

jemandem großen **Beifall** spenden 39

stürmischen **Beifall** ernten 86

sich die **Beine** vertreten, spazieren gehen 49

einen Knüppel zwischen die **Beine** werfen 142

wieder auf den **Beinen** sein 36

(ständig) auf den **Beinen** sein 36

mit beiden **Beinen** (fest) auf dem Boden stehen 36

auf eigenen **Beinen** stehen 36

das kommt mir **bekannt** vor, es erinnert mich an etwas 84

etwas noch **bereuen** 111

über den **Berg** sein, die schlimmste Zeit hinter sich haben 143

bergab gehen 143

jemanden **beruhigen** 106

eine schöne **Bescherung** 87

Register

jemanden **beschimpfen** 127

Ich fresse einen **Besen**, wenn 147

neue **Besen** kehren gut 84

jemanden spielend **besiegen** 65

sich anders **besinnen**/entscheiden 107

nichts **Besonderes** 86

Besserwisser 124

besser als nichts 73

retten, was zu retten ist, das **Beste** daraus machen 151

das **Beste** von allen sein 137

wer zahlt hat's zu **bestimmen** 114

leichte **Beute** sein 16

Beziehungen spielen lassen 89

sich ein **Bild** davon machen 87

jemanden ins **Bild** setzen 87

im **Bilde** sein, Bescheid wissen 88

auf der **Bildfläche** erscheinen, auftauchen 154

eine weiche **Birne** haben 44

etwas an der **Birne** haben, spinnen, verrückt sein 73

sich **blamieren**, sich lächerlich machen 129

ein unbeschriebenes **Blatt** sein 19

das **Blatt** hat sich gewendet 89

kein **Blatt** vor den Mund nehmen 136

das **Blaue** vom Himmel herunterlügen 58

auf den ersten **Blick** 131

auf den zweiten **Blick** 131

das **Blut** in den Adern zum Kochen bringen 24

Blut ist dicker als Wasser 24

jemandem liegt etwas im **Blut** 24

Blut und Wasser schwitzen 24

Das ist **Bockmist**/Scheiße 14

auf den **Boden** der Tatsachen kommen (oder jemanden zurückholen) 67

einen **Bock** schießen, einen dummen Fehler machen 59

jemanden ins **Bockshorn** jagen 69

dünn wie eine **Bohnenstange** 94

Bombengeschäft/-erfolg sein 157

im gleichen **Boot** sitzen 77

den **Braten** riechen 21

um den heißen **Brei** herumreden 137

sein **Brot**/seine Brötchen verdienen 71

sein Geld/**Brot** ehrlich verdienen 123

ein richtiger **Brummbär** sein 13

jemand ist wie ein offenes **Buch** 149

Register

ein übler **Bursche**, mieser Typ sein 119

spottbillig/für ein **Butterbrot** zu haben sein 155

C

eine faire **Chance**/Gewinnchance haben 158

D

Dampf ablassen 113

jemandem die **Daumen** drücken 38

Daumen nach oben/unten geben 57

Däumchen drehen 56

mit jemanden unter einer **Decke** stecken 39

vor Freude an die **Decke** springen 85

an die **Decke** gehen 88

zusammen durch **dick** und dünn gehen 113

Man kann nicht zwei **Dinge** auf einmal haben 71

wie vom **Donner** gerührt sein 16

doppelzüngig sein 34

der **Drachen** (für eine Frau) 157

einen **draufmachen**, versumpfen 90

einen **Dreck** darum kümmern 72

ein **Dritter** stört nur 128

jemanden unter **Druck** setzen 40

Dummerchen, Dummkopf, albern 124

jemanden über etwas im **Dunkeln** lassen 118

durch und durch schlecht sein 71

etwas **durch** und durch sein 38

durchdrehen 74

durcheinander sein 128

durchgefroren sein 93

sich gerade so **durchschlagen**, halten 124

E

das ist mir völlig **egal** 102

sich gleichen wie ein **Ei** dem anderen 74

(Person) wie aus dem **Ei** gepellt 132

Eile mit Weile 105

sich **einarbeiten**/sich (in etwas) auskennen 81

jemandem etwas **einfallen**, in den Sinn kommen 107

nur das **eine** (eins) im Kopf haben 119

eins und eins zusammenzählen 128

jemanden in etwas (genau) **einweihen** 82

auf **Eis** legen 68

Register

das **Eis** brechen 68

die Spitze des **Eisbergs** 134

das **Eisen** schmieden, solange es heiß ist 69

eiskalt sein 118

wie ein **Elefant** im Porzellanladen 13

aus einer Mücke einen **Elefanten** machen 144

in einem **Elfenbeinturm** sitzen/leben 120

seine **Ellbogen** gebrauchen 27

am **Ende** sein 92

am **Ende** seiner Kraft sein 113

Ende gut, alles gut 116

jemandem **entgegen** starren 34

sich **entschließen**, entscheiden 107

fest **entschlossen** sein, sich anstrengen etwas zu tun 107

sich daran **erinnern** 107

sich nicht genau an etwas **erinnern** 37

jemandem etwas **erlassen**, davon kommen lassen 141

in vollem **Ernst** 103

es **ernst** meinen 150

jemanden **erpressen** 124

jemanden zu Tode **erschrecken** 61

sich zu Tode **erschrecken** 55

auf frischer Tat **ertappt** werden 42

störrisch wie ein **Esel** 20

zittern wie **Espenlaub** 137

etwas an sich haben, das gewisse **Etwas** haben 66

Eulen nach Athen tragen 147

ewig nicht gesehen 140

bis in alle **Ewigkeit** 15

bis in alle **Ewigkeit** weitermachen 159

F

von seinem **Fach** reden, **fachsimpeln** 154

am seidenen **Faden** hängen 63

den **Faden** verlieren 63

den **Faden** wiederaufnehmen 63

sich in die **Falle** hauen, schlafen gehen 137

eine **Falle** stellen 160

etwas tun auf eigene **Faust** 76

Faustregel 56

nicht viel **Federlesen** machen 25

ein dickes **Fell** haben 55

seine **Felle** davon schwimmen sehen 95

weg vom **Fenster** sein 78

Geld aus dem **Fenster** geschmissen 122

jemandem dicht auf den **Fersen** sein 48

Register

damit spielend **fertig** werden 156

fertig ist der Lack! 124

ins **Fettnäpfchen** treten 35

mit dem **Feuer** spielen 68

Feuer und Flamme sein 73

fies aussehen, ein übler Mensch sein 156

eine gute **Figur** abgeben, sich gut schlagen 121

jemanden um den (kleinen) **Finger** wickeln 37

keinen **Finger** rühren/ krumm machen 37

sich die **Finger** wund arbeiten 38

sich wie ein **Fisch** auf dem Trockenen fühlen 17

ein kleiner **Fisch** 17

sich fühlen wie ein **Fisch** im Wasser 17

munter wie ein **Fisch** im Wasser, kerngesund sein 150

das sind kleine **Fische** 74

jemanden unter seine **Fittiche** nehmen 133

flachliegen 23

keiner **Fliege** etwas zuleide tun 17

zwei **Fliegen** mit einer Klappe schlagen 13

auf der **Flucht** sein 82

nicht in (seiner besten/ üblichen) **Form** sein 78

sei nicht so **frech** zu mir 26

die **Frechheit** haben, etwas zu tun 38

des einen **Freud**, des anderen Leid 73

sprühen vor **Freude** 70

sich **freuen**, jemanden von hinten zu sehen 23

dicke/enge **Freunde** sein 133

schlau wie ein **Fuchs** 18

jemanden unter seiner **Fuchtel** haben 56

mit einem **Fuß** im Grabe stehen 35

mit dem linken **Fuß** aufstehen 118

(festen) **Fuß** fassen 35

mit jemandem auf guten **Fuß** stehen 133

jemanden auf dem falschen **Fuß** erwischen 35

auf freiem **Fuß** sein, frei herumlaufen 159

kalte **Füße** bekommen/haben 36

immer auf die **Füße** fallen 36

jemanden den Boden unter den **Füßen** wegziehen 36

auf eigenen **Füßen** stehen, für seinen Unterhalt aufkommen 124

in jemandes **Fußstapfen** treten 35

Register

G

etwas in **Gang** halten 76

ganz und gar, mit Stumpf und Stil 159

aufs **Ganze** gehen 18

ein **Gedächtnis** wie ein Sieb 89

ein **Gedächtnis** wie ein Elefant haben 16

dem **Gedächtnis** entfallen 107

mit dem **Gedanken** spielen, etwas zu tun 105

jemanden auf dumme **Gedanken** bringen 44

seine **Gedanken** lesen 107

etwas darum geben, jemandes **Gedanken** lesen zu können 123

seine **Gedanken** beisammen haben/einen klaren Kopf haben 116

Gefahr für Leib und Leben sein 93

Gefallen finden an 103

seinen **Gefühlen** freien Lauf lassen 104

die zweite **Geige** spielen 150

den **Geist** aufgeben 97

von allen guten **Geistern** verlassen sein 112

ihm wurde **gekündigt** 77

gelb vor Neid sein 65

Geld wie Heu haben 88

Geld herausrücken, blechen 92

im **Geld** schwimmen 122

nicht für **Geld** und gute Worte, um keinen Preis 106

Geld aus dem Fenster geschmissen 122

Geld spielt keine Rolle 122

etwas für alles **Geld** der Welt nicht tun 76

nachgeworfenes **Geld** 72

sein **Geld**/Brot ehrlich verdienen 123

sein **Geld** wert sein 75

sich (beinah, fast) das **Genick** brechen, sich fast überschlagen 51

gerade zur rechten Zeit, gerade noch (rechtzeitig) 140

jemanden **gerecht** behandeln 151

es geht das **Gerücht** um 134

krumme Dinger drehen/faule **Geschäfte** machen 150

ein **Geschenk** des Himmels 104

etwas läuft wie **geschmiert** 85

der lange Arm des **Gesetzes** 151

sich (nicht) im Rahmen des **Gesetzes** bewegen 152

die Lücke des **Gesetzes**/ Gesetzeslücke 152

ein Schlag ins **Gesicht** für jemanden sein 31

ein langes **Gesicht** machen 33

sein **Gesicht** verlieren 33

sein **Gesicht** wahren 33

jemandem nicht ins **Gesicht** schauen können 33

jemandem ins **Gesicht** lachen 33

jemandem ins **Gesicht** lügen 33

jemandem etwas ins **Gesicht** sagen 33

jemandem steht etwas ins **Gesicht** geschrieben 34

sein wahres **Gesicht** zeigen 118

das zweite **Gesicht** haben, hellsehen können 113

jemandem wie aus dem **Gesicht** geschnitten sein, wie er leibt und lebt 131

sich zum **Gespött**/sich lächerlich machen 119

etwas im **Gespür** haben 25

das ist (alles) Schnee von **gestern** 142

gesund und munter ankommen 132

auf dem **Gewissen** haben 102

sein **Gewissen** beruhigen 108

eine **Gewissensfrage** sein 102

in seinen **Gewohnheiten** festgefahren sein 120

Gift darauf nehmen können 121

der **Gipfel** sein 138

jemanden auf **Glatteis** führen, an der Nase herum führen 87

ein **Glatzkopf** sein 91

im guten **Glauben** handeln, nach bestem Wissen 97

sich **gleichen** wie ein Ei dem anderen 74

das ist mir alles **gleich**, ist mit egal 111

Glück im Unglück haben 95

das **Glück** auf seiner Seite haben 99

(ironisch) noch nichts von seinem **Glück** wissen 99

unverschämtes **Glück** haben 99

von **Glück** sagen können/ sich glücklich schätzen 99

ein **Glückspilz** sein 15

ein Schatz/**Gold** wert sein, unschätzbar 122

wie **Gott** in Frankreich leben 48

in **Gottes** Namen, selbstverständlich 100

Um **Gottes**/Himmels willen! 106

es bringt/du bringst mich noch ins **Grab** 96

mit einem Fuß im **Grabe** stehen 35

ins **Gras** beißen 85

die **Grenze** ziehen 152

auf einen Schlag, in einem **Griff** 113

der **Groschen** ist gefallen 123

grün und blau schlagen 64

einer Sache auf den **Grund** gehen 101

alles spricht dafür, guten **Grund** haben zur Annahme, ... 110

gemäß seinen **Grundsätzen**/nach seinen Prinzipien leben 120

den **Gürtel** enger schnallen 59

jemandem ein Schlag unter die **Gürtellinie** versetzen 59

H

ein **Haar** in der Suppe 18

jemanden kein **Haar** krümmen 38

jemandem stehen die **Haare** zu Berge 39

sich in den **Haaren** liegen 46

Haarspalterei betreiben 39

sich die **Hacken** ablaufen (nach etwas), sich die **Hacken** abrennen 36

ohne **Haken** 89

halbe-halbe machen, mit jemandem etwas teilen 125

die bessere **Hälfte** 125

damit ist schon viel/die **Hälfte** gewonnen 157

seinen **Hals** riskieren 51

jemanden am **Hals** haben 22

genug/viel am **Hals** haben 88

bis zum **Hals** in Arbeit stecken 31

jemandem bleiben die Worte im **Halse** stecken 56

Wucher/**Halsabschneiderei** sein 144

jemandes rechte **Hand** sein 40

die **Hand** nicht beißen, die einen füttert 39

(bei etwas) die **Hand** im Spiel haben 40

die **Hand** gegen jemanden erheben 41

etwas aus erster/zweiter **Hand** hören 40

jemanden anfassen, **Hand** anlegen 37

etwas an einer **Hand** abzählen (können) 38

eine **Hand** wäscht die andere 22

jemandem zur **Hand** gehen 40

aus erster **Hand** 50

jemandem freie **Hand** lassen 40

von/aus der **Hand** in den Mund leben 40

es liegt in jemandes **Hand** 43

jemandem aus der **Hand** fressen 41

jemanden fest in der **Hand** haben 54

man kann die **Hand** nicht vor Augen sehen 52

zur **Hand** sein, in Reichweite sein 40

sich die **Hände** schmutzig machen 43

nur zwei **Hände** haben 43

jemandem in die **Hände** spielen 43

jemandem sind die **Hände** gebunden 43

alle **Hände** voll zu tun haben 42

zwei linke **Hände** haben 57

mit leeren **Händen** ausgehen 42

ein schlechter **Handel** 143

aus dem **Handgelenk**, aus dem Stegreif 60

das **Handtuch** werfen, die Flinte ins Korn werfen 90

Hans Dampf in allen Gassen 126

was **Hänschen** nicht lernt, lernt Hans nimmermehr 15

im **Handumdrehen** 41

wissen wie der **Hase** läuft/etwas auf dem Kasten haben 155

ein alter **Hase** in etwas sein 39

ein **Hasenfuß** sein 18

alles über den **Haufen** werfen 70

jemandem weit/**haushoch** überlegen sein 145

der Herr im **Haus** sein 144

sich wie zu **Hause** fühlen, es sich gemütlich machen 86

jemandem unter die **Haut** gehen 55

nur noch **Haut** und Knochen sein 54

jemandes/die eigene **Haut** retten 55

in jemandes **Haut** stecken 62

nicht in jemandes **Haut** stecken mögen 55

die nackte **Haut** retten 70

jemandem (nach oben) **helfen** 49

kein **Hemd** auf dem Leib tragen 62

es zu etwas bringen bzw. **herunterkommen** 148

eigener **Herd** ist Gold wert, daheim ist daheim 86

etwas **herunterspielen**, verharmlosen 81

ein goldenes **Herz** haben, gutherzig sein 47

das **Herz** am rechten Fleck haben 47

sein **Herz** an etwas/ jemanden hängen 47

sich etwas zu **Herzen** nehmen, zu Herzen gehen lassen 47

es nicht über das **Herz** bringen etwas zu tun 47

ein **Herz** aus Stein haben 47

(nicht) mit dem **Herzen** bei etwas sein 47

Register

seinem **Herzen** Luft machen, sich etwas von der Seele reden 26

gib deinem **Herzen** einen Stoß 48

etwas auf dem **Herzen** haben 107

etwas nach **Herzenslust** tun 48

eine sehr große **Hilfe** sein 41

wie der **Himmel** auf Erden sein 97

aus heiterem **Himmel** 64

im 7. **Himmel** sein 97

zum **Himmel** stinken 97

Um **Himmels** willen! 100

auf dasselbe **hinauslaufen** 111

sich in etwas **hineinknien**, festbeißen 58

das müßte eigentlich **hinhauen** 155

etwas in der **Hinterhand** haben 63

jeder **Hinz** und Kunz, jeder x-beliebige 128

Hochmut kommt vor dem Fall 109

ein **Hoffnungsschimmer** 110

seine **Hoffnung** darauf setzen 105

schwanger sein, guter **Hoffnung** 130

ein **hoffnungsloser** Fall sein 106

nicht auf der **Höhe** sein 92

den **Höhepunkt** erreichen, sich zuspitzen 44

jemandem die **Hölle** heiß machen 97

auf **Holz** klopfen, viel Glück 138

auf dem **Holzweg**/auf dem falschen Dampfer sein 139

Honig um den Bart schmieren 71

wie ein **Honigkuchenpferd** grinsen 14

kein **Honigschlecken** sein 74

seinen **Horizont**/Erfahrung erweitern, aufgeschlossener werden 108

die **Hosen** anhaben 64

das **Huhn**, das goldene Eier legt, schlachten 18

mit jemandem ein **Hühnchen** zu rupfen haben 25

mit den **Hühnern** aufstehen 20

auf den **Hund** gekommen sein 64

leben wie ein **Hund** 98

Da liegt der **Hund** begraben 138

schlafende **Hunde** soll man nicht wecken 16

bellende **Hunde** beißen nicht 129

sich **hundeelend** fühlen 67

sich etwas an den **Hut** stecken können 59

den **Hut** herumgehen lassen 61

vor jemandem/etwas den **Hut** ziehen 61

Register

I

jemanden **ignorieren**, schneiden 146

jemandes **Interesse** wecken, ihm gefallen 103

J

das ist **Jacke** wie Hose, dasselbe in Grün 128

die besten **Jahre** hinter sich haben 143

alle **Jubeljahre** (einmal) 64

das **juckt** mich überhaupt nicht 125

eine alte **Jungfer** sein 88

aus **Jux** und Tollerei 98

K

kalter **Kaffee** sein 16

kaltblütig handeln 24

harter **Kampf** sein 160

(Geld) auf die hohe **Kante** legen 122

etwas **kapieren**, raffen 106

alles auf eine **Karte** setzen 72

alle **Karten**/Trümpfe in der Hand haben/behalten 77

seine **Karten** offen auf dem Tisch legen, mit offenen Karten spielen 77

etwas/ jemanden fallenlassen wie eine heiße **Kartoffel** 75

getrennte **Kasse** machen 147

mit jemandem **Katz** und Maus spielen 14

die **Katze** aus dem Sack lassen 14

einen **Katzensprung**/Steinwurf entfernt 89

der **Kern** der Sache 47

kerngesund sein, in bester Verfassung 93

ein gebranntes **Kind** scheut das Feuer 101

das **Kind**/die Dinge beim (rechten) Namen nennen 142

kinderleicht 74

arm wie eine **Kirchenmaus** 20

ein **Klacks**, ein Kinderspiel 71

jemandem etwas **klarmachen** 86

in einer **Klasse** für sich sein, unvergleichbar sein 102

das **Kleingedruckte** lesen 153

jemandem aus der **Klemme** helfen 141

in der **Klemme**/Patsche sitzen/sein 141

einen **Kloß** im Hals haben 56

kneifen 15

jemanden nicht einmal mit der **Kneifzange** anfassen 81

in der **Kneipe** hocken 142

einen **Knüppel** zwischen die Beine werfen 142

Register

auf glühenden **Kohlen** sitzen 15

unbeschreiblich **komisch** 136

wer zuerst **kommt**, mahlt zuerst 13

auf **Komplimente** aus sein 102

geeignet/gut genug für einen **König** 158

außer **Kontrolle** geraten 41

sich über etwas den **Kopf** zerbrechen 25

einen kühlen **Kopf** bewahren 44

den **Kopf** verlieren 44

sich etwas in den **Kopf** setzen 45

sich etwas aus dem **Kopf** schlagen 45

jemandem will etwas nicht in den **Kopf** gehen 45

etwas nicht aus dem **Kopf** bekommen 108

mit dem **Kopf** gegen die Wand rennen 45

sich mit dem **Kopf** über Wasser halten 45

etwas steigt jemandem zu **Kopf** 44

einen klaren **Kopf** haben 117

jemandem den **Kopf** verdrehen 46

jemandem wachsen die Dinge über den **Kopf** 114

Kopf an Kopf 51

sich **kopfüber** in eine Sache stürzen 130

am Ende seiner **Kraft** sein 113

jemandem an den **Kragen** wollen 24

kreidebleich, leichenblass sein 65

in **Kreisen** reden, sich im Kreise drehen 130

das **Kriegsbeil** begraben 158

mit jemandem auf **Kriegsfuß** stehen 158

auf dem **Kriegspfad** sein 160

als **Krönung** des Ganzen 121

Das ist die **Krönung**, das ist die Höhe 60

ein Stück vom **Kuchen** (wollen) 71

hinter den **Kulissen** 154

jemandem **kündigen**, jemanden herausschmeißen 59

Was macht die **Kunst**? 155

besondere **Kunstgriffe**, Geschäftskniffe 155

um es **kurz** und bündig zu sagen 74

L

sich **totlachen** 46

ins **Lächerliche** ziehen 79

den **Laden** schmeißen 154

sich in jemandes **Lage** versetzen 62

in einer gefährlichen **Lage** sein 93

etwas geduldig wie ein **Lamm** ertragen 19

sanft wie ein **Lamm** 20

unschuldig wie ein (neugeborenes) **Lamm** 131

Lampenfieber haben 14

andere **Länder**, andere Sitten 148

langsam aber sicher 113

sich etwas durch die **Lappen** gehen lassen 38

viel **Lärm** um nichts 129

Das muss man ihm **lassen** 41

mit seinem **Latein**/seiner Weisheit am Ende sein 117

jemanden auf dem **Laufenden** halten 88

auf dem **Laufenden** bleiben 118

sich wie ein **Lauffeuer** verbreiten 67

um sein **Leben** rennen 98

sein **Leben** aufs Spiel setzen 43

jemandem sein **Leben** retten, die nackte Haut retten 70

Gefahr für Leib und **Leben** sein, lebensgefährlich sein 93

sich mit **Leib** und Seele einer Sache widmen 48

leben und leben lassen 99

nie im **Leben** 139

ein neues **Leben** anfangen, ein neues Kapitel aufschlagen 137

in voller **Lebensgröße** 98

ein **Leckermaul** sein 58

sich jemanden vom **Leibe** halten, auf Distanz halten 22

nur über meine **Leiche** 25

(Es ist) **leichter** gesagt als getan 111

man **lernt** nie aus 99

den kann man nicht hinters **Licht** führen 17

etwas in einem anderen **Licht** zeigen 99

mit der Entfernung wächst die **Liebe** 100

etwas mit **links** machen 22

mit **links** gewinnen 43

Lippenbekenntnis ablegen 49

saufen wie ein **Loch** 17

aus dem letzten **Loch** pfeifen 49

auf seinen **Lorbeeren** ausruhen 119

der **Löwenanteil** 20

die **Lücke** des Gesetzes/ Gesetzeslücke 152

in die **Luft** gehen, an die Decke gehen 66

jemandem nicht die **Luft** zum Atmen gönnen 66

Es herrscht dicke **Luft** 66

Es liegt etwas in der **Luft** 66

Register

aus der **Luft** (greifen) 66

die **Luft** ist rein 130

Lunte riechen/den Braten riechen 21

M

ein **Machtwort** sprechen, jemanden zeigen, wo es langgeht 35

etwas dreht jemanden den **Magen** um 55

jemanden in (durch) die **Mangel** nehmen (drehen) 156

ein **Mann** der zu seinem Wort steht 135

den **Märtyrer** spielen, sich aufopfern 119

meckern, nörgeln 70

jemandem gründlich seine **Meinung** sagen, jemandem sagen, wo es lang geht 105

seine **Meinung** äußern, frei herausreden 108

jemandem ordentlich die **Meinung** sagen 108

keine **Miene** verziehen 33

im **Mittelpunkt** stehen, im Rampenlicht stehen 152

Morgen ist auch noch ein Tag 140

spielend/ohne **Mühe**/mit links gewinnen 43

sich (große) **Mühe** geben, etwas zu tun 93

sich besondere **Mühe** geben/ keine Mühen scheuen 115

Halt den **Mund**, hör auf! 63

jemandem läuft das Wasser in **Mund** zusammen 50

von **Mund** zu Mund 50

kein Blatt vor dem **Mund** nehmen 136

jemandem die Worte in den **Mund** legen 50

jemandem das Wort aus dem **Mund** nehmen 50

nicht auf den **Mund** gefallen sein 104

den **Mund** halten, sich zurückhalten 57

jemandem etwas mit gleicher **Münze** heimzahlen, gleiches mit Gleichem vergelten 93

den **Mut** haben, etwas zu tun 38

den **Mut** verlieren 48

seinen ganzen **Mut** zusammennehmen 141

angetrunkener **Mut** 147

mutig wie ein Löwe 20

N

der **Nachahmer** sein 130

einen bitteren **Nachgeschmack** hinterlassen 50

bis spät in die **Nacht** arbeiten, Nachtschicht einlegen 74

mitten in der **Nacht** 96

Nägel mit Köpfen machen, Ärmel hochkrempeln 37

Register

ein **Nagel** zu jemandes Sarg sein 141

den **Nagel** auf den Kopf treffen 141

sich einen **Namen** machen, sein Ziel erreichen 79

jemandes guten **Namen** in den Schmutz ziehen, jemanden öffentlich schlecht machen 126

jemanden zum **Narren** halten 20

eine **Naschkatze** sein 58

Nase voll von etwas/ jemandem haben 24

jemanden vor der **Nase** wegfahren 32

auf die **Nase** fallen 34

jemandem die Tür vor der **Nase** zuschlagen 34

über etwas die **Nase** rümpfen 52

jemandem etwas vor der **Nase** wegschnappen 52

immer der **Nase** nach 53

in alles seine **Nase** stecken 52

jemandem eine (lange) **Nase** zeigen 53

jemanden mit der **Nase** auf etwas stoßen 53

jemanden an der **Nase** herumführen 53

seine **Nase** in etwas hineinstecken 53

jemandem etwas unter die **Nase** reiben 53

die **Nase** vorn haben 118

sich eine goldene **Nase** verdienen 122

etwas an jemandes **Nasenspitze** erkennen 32

jemandem zur zweiten **Natur** geworden sein 68

vor **Neid** aufgefressen werden 119

gelb vor **Neid** sein 65

die **Nerven**/den Mut verlieren 51

jemandem auf die **Nerven**/ den Wecker gehen 52

mit den **Nerven** am Ende sein 95

ein **Nervenbündel** sein 95

eine **Nervensäge** sein 51

sei **nett**!/gib deinem Herzen einen Stoß 48

neugierige Leute sterben früh 15

besser als **nichts** 73

nichts für ungut 104

nichts verraten 135

niedergeschlagen sein 103

eine **Notlüge** erzählen 105

in **null** Komma nichts, im Nu 126

eine harte **Nuss** zu knacken sein 74

Register

O

die **Oberhand** haben/gewinnen 41

unvoreingenommen sein, **offen** für etwas sein 120

Ohne mich!/Da mache ich nicht mit! 124

ein feines **Ohr**/Gehör für etwas haben 26

zum einem **Ohr** hinein, zum andern (wieder) hinaus 26

ganz **Ohr** sein 27

jemanden übers **Ohr** hauen, aufs Glatteis führen 111

über beide **Ohren** grinsen 32

noch grün hinter den **Ohren** sein 27

bis über die/über beide **Ohren** in (Schulden) stecken 27

seinen **Ohren** nicht trauen 27

jemandem zu **Ohren** kommen 27

die **Ohren** spitzen 27

über beide **Ohren** grinsen 32

bis über beide **Ohren** verliebt sein 44

Musik in jemandes **Ohren** sein 153

die **Ohren** steif halten 26

Öl ins Feuer gießen 85

wie die **Ölsardinen** 75

frech wie **Oskar**, unverschämt sein 118

Otto Normalverbraucher, Durchschnittsbürger 144

P

die Wände hochgehen, auf die **Palme** bringen 90

unter dem **Pantoffel** stehen 18

was **passiert** ist, ist passiert; hin ist hin 73

auf die **Pauke** hauen 145

eine gespaltene **Persönlichkeit** haben 126

wer den **Pfennig** nicht ehrt, ist des Talers nicht wert; spar im Kleinen, dann hast Du im Großen 123

keinen **Pfennig** (in der Tasche) haben 123

völlig pleite sein, keinen **Pfennig** besitzen 123

das **Pferd** beim Schwanze aufzäumen 19

aufs falsche **Pferd** setzen 19

wie ein **Pferd** arbeiten 19

phantastisch, himmlisch sein 148

von der **Pike** auf dienen, lernen 156

wie aus der **Pistole** geschossen, blitzschnell 159

sich fehl am **Platz** fühlen/sein 147

kaum **Platz** haben, sich zu rühren 14

Register

das klingt **plausibel** 112

auf verlorenem **Posten** stehen/kämpfen 157

für den **Preis** geschenkt sein 121

um keinen **Preis** 106

kurzen **Prozess** machen mit etwas 156

ein wunder **Punkt** sein 109

einen toten **Punkt** haben 109

Q

Quatsch, dummes Zeug reden 61

R

sich **rächen** 23

das fünfte **Rad** am Wagen sein 72

mit seinen Kräften **Raubbau** treiben, sich übernehmen 85

sie können mit mir **rechnen** 124

die **Rechnung** bezahlen 35

das **Recht** selbst in die Hand nehmen 152

vom **Regen** in die Traufe kommen 87

in **Reichweite** sein 40

jetzt bist du an der **Reihe** 76

jemanden **reinwaschen**, decken 65

sich an die **Regeln** halten 57

im **Rennen** (für etwas) liegen/sein 82

retten was zu **retten** ist, das Beste daraus machen 151

genau das **Richtige** 93

Das ist genau das **Richtige**, ideal 92

den richtigen **Riecher** für etwas haben 52

sich am **Riemen** reißen 63

am **Rockzipfel** der Mutter hängen 129

die/seine **Rolle** spielen als 153

die **Rolle** passt zu jemandem 153

keine **Rose** ohne Dornen 138

etwas hinter jemandes **Rücken** tun 23

jemandem den **Rücken** zudrehen 23

mit dem **Rücken** an der Wand stehen, in die Enge getrieben sein 23

es läuft jemandem eiskalt über den **Rücken** 24

kein **Rückgrat** haben 23

einen **Rückzieher** machen 76

seinem **Ruf** gerecht werden 120

einen guten/schlechten **Ruf** haben 126

jemanden in **Ruhe** lassen 23

Nicht so schnell! Immer mit der **Ruhe**! 19

Register

die **Ruhe** vor dem Sturm 69

keine **Ruhe** haben, keinen Seelenfrieden haben 109

seelenruhig/die **Ruhe** selbst sein 72

ein **Ruhmesblatt** für jemanden sein 17

die letzte **Runde** trinken (in einer Kneipe/Party) 144

S

eine **Sache**/die Atmosphäre bereinigen 67

nicht jemandes **Sache** sein 76

keine halben **Sachen** machen 125

ihn (im eigenen **Saft**) schmoren lassen 75

Salz in die Wunde streuen 75

es mehr als **satt** haben 58

jemanden/etwas **satt** haben 101

(fest) im **Sattel** sitzen 82

sauber bleiben 54

in **Saus** und Braus leben 72

in **Schach** halten, (provisorisch) hinhalten 77

aus dem eigenen **Schaden** lernen/ klug werden 115

etwas leicht/spielend **schaffen** 82

selten ein **Schaden** ohne Nutzen 67

die **Schafe** von den Böcken trennen 21

eine **Schande** sein 112

zu allen **Schandtaten** bereit sein 78

die **Schau** stehlen, im Mittelpunkt stehen 154

einen **Schaufensterbummel** machen 146

sich von jemandem eine **Scheibe** abschneiden 137

fressen wie ein **Scheunendrescher** 19

klar **Schiff** machen/sich bereit machen 130

das sinkende **Schiff** verlassen 132

keinen **Schimmer**/Dunst von etwas haben 105

schlafen wie ein Stein 138

Das war ein **Schlag** ins Gesicht für jemanden 31

ein **Schlag** ins Wasser sein 131

ein **Schlag** ins Gesicht für jemanden sein 32

auf einen **Schlag**, in einem Griff 113

jemanden **schlagen** 43

mit jemandem eine **Schlägerei** haben 159

jemanden **schlecht** gehen, in schlechter Verfassung sein 94

jemanden **schlechtmachen**/ runtermachen 82

alles noch **schlimmer** machen 119

hinter **Schloss** und Riegel halten 141

Register

ein **Schlummertrunk** 60

das ist (alles) **Schnee** von gestern 142

sich wie ein **Schneekönig** freuen 65

Schönheit liegt im Auge des Betrachters 129

jemanden in seine **Schranken** weisen 147

einen **Schritt** voraus sein 79

zusammenpassen wie ein Paar alte **Schuhe** 86

die **Schuld** auf sich nehmen 54

über jemandes **Schulter** schauen 51

jemandem die kalte **Schulter** zeigen 54

jemandem auf die **Schulter** klopfen 23

unfehlbarer **Schütze** 159

Schwamm drüber/die Vergangenheit ruhen lassen 101

warten bis man **schwarz** wird 64

ins **Schwarze** treffen 80

den **schwarzen** Peter haben 129

ganz zu **schweigen** von 134

schweigsamer Mensch, nicht viel Worte machen 136

ein Vermögen/**Schweinegeld** kosten 157

voll in **Schwung** sein 159

sich etwas von der **Seele** reden 25

Seemannsgarn erzählen/ spinnen 64

sich **sehen** lassen, auftauchen 34

sich nach jemanden sehr **sehnen** 91

wie dem auch **sei** 134

Das ist doch **selbstverständlich** 156

weggehen wie warme **Semmeln** 71

in **Sicherheit** bringen/ stellen 115

ein Gedächtnis wie ein **Sieb** 89

alles/es macht plötzlich **Sinn**, sich zusammenfügen 147

jemanden etwas einfallen, in den **Sinn** kommen 107

seine fünf **Sinne** nicht beisammen haben 112

nicht bei **Sinnen** sein, verrückt sein 112

keine **Skrupel**/Bedenken haben 110

jemanden von den **Socken** reißen 37

jemanden verdächtigen/ **spanisch** vorkommen 17

Spar im Kleinen, dann hast Du im Großen 123

Spare in der Zeit, so hast du in der Not 115

Spaß beiseite 131

Register

lieber den **Spatz** in der Hand als die Taube auf dem Dach 13

aufgeben, das **Spiel** verloren geben 42

sein Leben aufs **Spiel** setzen 43

ein leichtes **Spiel** haben 78

gute Miene zum bösen **Spiel** machen 121

jemandem sein **Spiel** verderben 78

das **Spiel** ist aus 78

(bei etwas) die Hand im **Spiel** haben 40

sein **Spiel** mit jemandem treiben 79

alles aufs **Spiel** setzen 83

auf dem **Spiel** stehen 83

um die Ehre **spielen**, zum Spaß spielen 81

nach den Regeln/ehrlich **spielen** 79

spielend/ohne Mühe/mit links gewinnen 43

fairer/ehrlicher **Spieler**, guter/schlechter Verlierer sein 83

ein **Spielverderber** sein 16

man kann den **Spieß** auch umdrehen 78

den **Spieß** umdrehen, das Blatt wenden 90

ganz **spontan** 83

Sprache verlieren/wieder finden 57

sprachlos sein 136

ein **Sprung** ins kalte Wasser 79

auf einen **Sprung** (vorbei) kommen 132

sprunghaft 79

jemanden von der **Spur** abbringen 112

jemandem/etwas auf der **Spur** sein 145

auf der richtigen/falschen **Spur** sein 145

spurlos verschwinden 66

Stadtgespräch sein 145

hart wie **Stahl**, knallhart 141

von der **Stange** (etwas kaufen) 80

einen schlechten **Start** haben 35

eine **Stecknadel** fallen hören 88

eine **Stecknadel** im Heuhaufen suchen 144

Da **steckt** mehr dahinter 31

jemanden ein **Stein** vom Herzen fallen, sein Gewissen beruhigen 108

schlafen wie ein **Stein** 138

an die **Stelle** treten von jemanden, ihn ersetzen 147

abrupt stehen bleiben, plötzlich auf der **Stelle** stehen bleiben 146

Register

etwas auf der **Stelle**/ohne Weiteres machen 61

Stellen Sie sich vor! Das gibt's doch nicht! 134

die **Stellung** halten 158

einer Sache seinen **Stempel** aufdrücken, seine Spur hinterlassen 80

jemanden im **Stich** lassen, hängen lassen 105

jemandem die **Stiefel** lecken 60

Das sind zwei verschiedene Paar **Stiefel** 63

den **Stier** bei den Hörnern packen 14

stocknüchtern sein 151

stocktaub sein 92

stolz wie ein Pfau/Spanier 21

seinen **Stolz** überwinden, klein beigeben 109

stolz auf etwas sein 110

stolze Summe sein/bezahlen 123

am selben/gleichen **Strang** ziehen 157

über die **Stränge** schlagen, zu weit gehen 80

auf der **Strecke** bleiben, scheitern 94

keinen **Strich** machen 83

ein **Strich** in der Landschaft sein 94

auf den **Strich** gehen 145

unter dem **Strich**/das Entscheidende/alles in allem 152

jemandem aus etwas einen **Strick** zu drehen 115

ein **Strohfeuer**, einmaliger Erfolg 87

mit/gegen den **Strom** schwimmen 83

es gießt in **Strömen**, wie aus Eimern/Kübeln/Kannen 68

Die **Stunde** hat geschlagen 90

die Ruhe vor dem **Sturm** 69

ein **Sturm** im Wasserglas 69

jemandem die **Suppe** versalzen 78

die **Suppe** auslöffeln, die Folgen tragen 153

ein Haar in der **Suppe** 18

T

Man soll den **Tag** nicht vor dem Abend loben 15

jemandem den **Tag** retten/versüßen 139

Morgen ist auch noch ein **Tag** 140

jemandes **Tage**/Stunden sind gezählt 127

am helllichten **Tage** 139

Tapetenwechsel, Luftveränderung brauchen 154

sich **tapfer** zur Wehr setzen, sich tapfer/mutig wehren 158

Register

etwas so gut wie in der **Tasche** haben 59

tief in die **Tasche** greifen 54

etwas schon in der **Tasche** haben 62

jemanden auf der **Tasche** liegen, schnorren 89

jemanden in die **Tasche** stecken/ jemandem weit überlegen sein 159

Taten sprechen lassen 122

den **Tatsachen** ins Auge sehen, sich einer Sache stellen 32

sich **taub** stellen 26

taufrisch/quicklebendig sein 137

seinen **Teil** dazu beitragen, dabei helfen 153

der **Teufel** ist los 72

Wenn man vom **Teufel** spricht, kommt er auch 96

zum **Teufel** mit etwas 98

Geh zum **Teufel**, du kannst mich mal 98

Theater spielen 149

ein großes **Tier** 17

in der **Tinte** sitzen, in der Klemme stecken 75

reinen **Tisch** machen, aufräumen 84

tipptopp, in Ordnung 132

jemanden zu **Tode** erschrecken 132

sich zu **Tode** erschrecken 55

jemanden zu **Tode** langweilen 61

sich zu **Tode** langweilen 101

sich den **Tod** holen 92

mit dem **Tode** ringen 92

todmüde/fertig sein 95

zu **Tode** arbeiten 96

jemanden einen **Todesschrecken** einjagen 117

sein eigenes **Todesurteil** unterzeichnen 96

Das ist **todsicher** 86

etwas in einem netten **Ton** sagen, höflich bleiben 57

neugierig/ein **Topfgucker** sein 54

tot und begraben sein, darüber ist längst Gras gewachsen 96

jemanden auf **Trab** halten 57

(dauernd) auf **Trab** sein, auf den Beinen sein 84

Wäre mir nicht im **Traum** eingefallen 103

die ganze **Trickkiste** 155

anfangen zu **trinken**/saufen 84

Das ist der **Tropfen**, der das Faß zum Überlaufen bringt 138

(nur) ein **Tropfen** auf den heißen Stein 68

im (alltäglichen) **Trott** sein 82

jemandem die **Tür** vor der Nase zuschlagen 34

Register

U

sich **übereilen**, voreilig sein 79

überglücklich sein 148

überschnappen, durchdrehen 74

Übertreibs mal nicht 73

Übung macht den Meister 153

die **Uhr** nicht zurückdrehen können 85

seine **Uhr** ist abgelaufen, seine Tage sind gezählt 140

ungeschickt/unfähig sein 42

jemanden **ungeschoren** davon kommen lassen 159

(Ein) **Unglück** kommt selten allein 68

unpässlich sein 65

für **Unruhe** sorgen 77

jemandes **Unschuld** beweisen 126

die **Unverschämtheit** haben 52

nichts **unversucht** lassen 89

unvoreingenommen sein, offen für etwas sein 120

sich (sehr) **unwohl** fühlen 93

uralt, steinalt 143

ein vorschnelles **Urteil** fällen 151

V

wie der **Vater**, so der Sohn 130

nicht zu **verachten** 94

die **Vergangenheit** ruhen lassen 101

sich **vergeblich** anstrengen 19

nicht zu **vergleichen** mit 144

über seine **Verhältnisse** leben 99

hart **verhandeln**, mächtig rangehen 121

ein **Vermögen**/Schweinegeld kosten 157

ein **Vermögen** bezahlen 67

auf die Stimme der **Vernuft** hören 111

zur **Vernunft** kommen 112

jemanden zur **Vernunft**/ Besinnung bringen 112

es/alles **verraten** 154

verrückt sein, spinnen, etwas an der Birne haben 73

jemanden wahnsinnig/ **verrückt** machen 109

jemanden in **Verruf** bringen 127

versessen auf etwas sein 98

(nicht) bei vollen **Verstand** sein 108

den **Verstand** verlieren, seine fünf Sinne nicht beisammen haben 112

den **Verstand** verloren haben 117

jemanden um seinen **Verstand** bringen 117

Es geht über meinen **Verstand** 100

etwas völlig missdeuten/ falsch **verstehen** 117

Register

durch **Versuch** und Irrtum lernen 133

etwas (mal) **versuchen**/ausprobieren 160

Das hat mir jemand im **Vertrauen** gesagt 13

ein Wort im **Vertrauen** 27

jemandem blind **vertrauen** 34

nach allen Regeln der Kunst (prächtig) **verwöhnen** 157

damit ist schon **viel**/die Hälfte gewonnen 157

eine **Vitaminspritze** 160

das hat mir ein **Vögelchen** gezwitschert 13

aneinander **vorbei** reden 110

sich **vordrängen** 153

sich an die **Vorschriften** halten 149

Vorsicht ist besser als Nachsicht 111

der **Vorsitz** einer Versammlung sein/den Vorsitz übernehmen 150

eine bestimmte **Vorstellung** haben/beabsichtigen 108

seinen **Vorteil** daraus ziehen 121

vorwärts kommen 46

Voyeur, Spanner 128

W

jemanden mit seinen eignen **Waffen** schlagen 79

keine **Wahl** haben, friss oder stirb 125

den **Wald** vor lauter Bäumen nicht sehen 138

Da wackelt die **Wand** 85

gegen eine **Wand** reden 90

mit dem Rücken an der **Wand** stehen 23

mit dem Kopf gegen die **Wand** rennen 45

die **Wände** hochgehen, auf die Palme bringen 90

die andere **Wange** hinhalten 26

etwas ins **Wanken** bringen, für Unruhe sorgen 77

jemanden/sich mit dem Kopf über **Wasser** halten 45

ein Sprung ins kalte **Wasser** 79

ein Schlag ins **Wasser** sein 131

stille **Wasser** sind tief 69

jemanden ins kalte **Wasser** werfen 130

Seitdem ist viel **Wasser** den Rhein/dem Fluß hinuntergeflossen 143

ein Sturm im **Wasserglas** 69

aussehen, als ob man kein **Wässerchen** trüben könnte 71

jemandem den **Weg** ebnen 115

weg vom Fenster sein 78

Es führt kein **Weg** daran vorbei 116

Alle/Viele **Wege** führen nach Rom 148

Register

Es tut mir alles **weh** 91

sich tapfer zur **Wehr** setzen 158

nicht **weichen**/nachgeben, festbleiben 158

weise wie eine Eule 21

(inzwischen) sehr **weit** gekommen 156

zu **weit** gehen, überreagieren 114

bei **weitem** nicht 160

ohne **weiteres** machen 61

bis in alle Ewigkeit **weitermachen** 159

Was in aller **Welt** ... 67

nicht um alles in der **Welt**, um keinen Preis 148

etwas für alles Geld der **Welt** nicht tun 76

davon geht die **Welt** nicht unter 148

in seiner eigenen (kleinen) **Welt** leben 148

falsch zu **Werke** gehen, verkehrten Ansatz verfolgen 115

sein Geld **wert** sein 75

wenig **Wert** auf Etikette legen 157

eine reine/saubere **Weste** haben 89

wie meine **Westentasche** kennen, in und auswendig kennen 42

nichts **Wichtiges**/Besonderes 86

ein **Wildfang** sein 128

seinen eigenen **Willen** haben, wissen was man will 120

etwas beim besten **Willen** nicht tun 100

seinen **Willen** durchsetzen 120

ohne mit der **Wimper** zu zucken 31

nicht mit der **Wimper** zucken 31

von etwas **Wind** bekommen 70

jemandem den **Wind** aus den Segeln nehmen 70

in den **Wind** reden 101

nicht **wissen** wohin (man sich wenden soll) 116

schwacher/alter **Witz** 131

die **Wogen** glätten 74

auf **Wolke** Sieben schweben/im 7. Himmel sein 97

über den **Wolken** schweben 46

in **Wolkenkuckucksheim** leben 146

ein **Wort** im Vertrauen 27

überhaupt nicht zu **Wort** kommen 134

ein gutes **Wort** für jemanden einlegen 135

sein **Wort** halten 135

jemandem das **Wort** aus dem Mund nehmen 50

sein **Wort** brechen 135

Register

das letzte **Wort** haben/behalten 135

ein Mann, der zu seinem **Wort** steht 135

aber kein **Wort** darüber 135

Eine Tat zählt mehr als 1000 **Worte** 100

sein (Ehren)**Wort** geben 136

nicht für Geld und gute **Worte** 106

jemandem die **Worte** in den Mund legen 50

jemandem bleiben die **Worte** im Halse stecken 56

seine **Worte** zurücknehmen (müssen) 136

mit **Worten** spielen, ein Wortspiel machen 81

blind vor **Wut** sein 91

in **Wut** geraten, einen Wutanfall haben 110

X

jemandem etwas **x-mal**/zigmal sagen 127

Z

die **Zähne** zusammenbeißen 58

bis an die **Zähne** bewaffnet sein 59

ein **Zankapfel** 25

streng im **Zaum** halten 42

zwischen den **Zeilen** lesen 152

seiner **Zeit** voraus sein 118

die schlimmste **Zeit** hinter sich haben 143

die verlorene **Zeit** einholen/gutmachen 140

gerade zu rechten **Zeit**, gerade noch (rechtzeitig) 140

die **Zeit** heilt alle Wunden 140

die **Zeit** totschlagen 140

keine **Zeit** daran verschwenden, kurzen Prozess machen mit etwas 156

die **Zeit** vergessen 145

jemanden ein bisschen mehr **Zeit** lassen 97

Spare in der **Zeit**, so hast Du in der Not 115

Zeter und Mordio schreien 65

nah/näher am **Ziel** sein 80

sein **Ziel** erreichen 79

weit vom **Ziel** sein, am Ziel vorbei 80

Zivilcourage haben 118

wer **zuerst** kommt, mahlt zuerst 125

zufällig 91

etwas dem **Zufall** überlassen 95

sich mit wenigem **zufrieden** geben 100

den **Zug**/den Anschluss verpassen 77

sich zuviel **zumuten** 71

Register

sich etwas auf der **Zunge** zergehen lassen 50

etwas liegt jemandem auf der **Zunge** 58

sich **zurechtfinden** 37

sich **zurückhalten** 57

jemanden **zutexten**, vollreden 49

zusammen durch dick und dünn gehen, **zusammenhalten** wie Pech und Schwefel 113

Zweifel haben an 114

Als Ergänzung empfehlen wir:

Problemlos sprechen – schnell verstehen

Unterwegs auf Urlaub in Großbritannien oder in den USA? Dann sollten Sie die wichtigsten Wörter und Wendungen beherrschen: Wo ist der Flughafen? Wie komme ich zum Hotel? Wie viel kostet das? Ob in der Pension, beim Einkaufsbummel, im Restaurant oder bei Behörden: Die richtigen Worte helfen weiter!

- thematisch geordneter Wortschatz
- Aussprachehilfe in internationaler Lautschrift
- Kurzgrammatik und Reisewörterbuch
- praktisches Format für die Tasche

Unterwegs in England

192 Seiten, robustes Flexcover
ISBN 978-3-8112-2582-4

Fit für das internationale Business: Hier sind alle wichtigen englischen Wörter und Wendungen zu finden, die beim Umgang mit Kunden und Geschäftspartnern unerlässlich sind. Neben umfangreichen Wortlisten und Beispielsätzen bietet der kompakte Ratgeber hilfreiche Tipps und Regeln für einen jederzeit kompetenten und souveränen Auftritt – egal, ob am Telefon, in der schriftlichen Korrespondenz, bei der Auftragsannahme und -vergabe, beim Messebesuch, in Meetings oder beim Smalltalk.

Birgit Adam
Business-Englisch
Smalltalk, Korrespondenz, Verhandlungen

192 Seiten, Flexcover
ISBN 978-3-8112-2860-3